CONFRONTATIONS
WITH
PROPHETS

OTHER FORTRESS PRESS BOOKS BY HANS WALTER WOLFF

Amos the Prophet: The Man and His Background
Anthropology of the Old Testament
Hosea (Hermeneia)
Joel and Amos (Hermeneia)
Micah the Prophet
The Old Testament: A Guide to Its Writings

CONFRONTATIONS WITH PROPHETS

Discovering the Old Testament's New and Contemporary Significance

HANS WALTER WOLFF

FORTRESS
PRESS
Philadelphia

Translated from the German *Prophetische Alternativen: Entdeckungen des Neuen im Alten Testament* by Hans Walter Wolff, copyright © 1982 Chr. Kaiser Verlag, München.

——————

Library of Congress Cataloging in Publication Data

Wolff, Hans Walter.
  Confrontations with prophets.

  Translation of: Prophetische Alternativen.
  1. Prophets—Addresses, essays, lectures. I. Title.
BS1198.W6413 1983   224'.06   82-21019
ISBN 0-8006-1702-9

——————

9773J82   Printed in the United States of America   1-1702

CONTENTS

Preface   7

1. The Irresistible Word   9
   Amos and the Well-deserved End

2. The Effective Word   22
   Hosea and the Healing of the Incorrigible

3. The Unmasking Word   35
   Micah and the Pious Leadership Circles

4. What is New in the New Covenant?   49
   *A Contribution to the Jewish-Christian Dialogue
   According to Jer. 31:31–34*

5. How Can We Recognize False Prophets?   63
   *Criteria for the Difficult Task of
   Testing the Spirits*

PREFACE

THE CHAPTERS THAT FOLLOW represent an attempt to sketch some major prophetic themes as these are illustrated in a few of the classical prophets. Prophecy does not simply perpetuate the assured faith of ancient Israel; on the contrary, it broaches a wholly new alternative. The very form of prophecy compels a certain fascination and, for us, raises questions about our own current forms of proclamation. This becomes clear in the cases of Amos, Hosea, and Micah. For us, what they present is at once both perfectly familiar and utterly strange. They are moved at least as much as we by the relationship between future and present, whereas for us this means an overriding sense of anxiety and peril, the prophets awaken insight into guilt and punishment (the consequence of guilt). From Amos on, the end becomes an irrepressible theme—for Israel, for the gentiles, and even for the individual. Hosea experiences and ponders the radical incorrigibility of human beings on the one hand, and on the other he sees and proclaims how human recalcitrance will be overcome by the transforming power of God's love. Micah relentlessly unmasks the piety that leaves human relationships untouched. The old covenant/new covenant distinction (Jeremiah 31) leads Jewish-Christian dialogue out of its impasse and inspires pursuit of the prophetic proclamation of the radically new as a path toward mutual understanding. The antithesis between true prophecy and false prophecy demands clarification of the question of how false prophets are to be known and exposed. A practical introduction is offered on knowing the false prophets. It is tested in the controversy about rearmament and peace.

Wherever readers encounter that which is distinctive in classical prophecy, they see themselves confronted by an inescapable choice, an option different from that of both preprophetic Israel and our own present-day positions and slogans. Already within the framework of the Old Testament itself prophecy incessantly produces not just something fresh, but the new as such. Prophecy comes to light as the indispensable presupposition for the New Testament message.

The chapters that follow presuppose the results of contemporary research on the prophets (research to which I have myself been contributing with my commentaries on Hosea, Joel, Amos, Obadiah, Jonah, and Micah). At the same time, however, as public lectures addressed to students, ministers, and other interested persons, they point up the continuing relevance of the prophets for theology and preaching today.

I thank sincerely Margaret Kohl, Thomas Trapp, and Ralph Gehrke for aid in the work of translation.

1

THE IRRESISTIBLE WORD

Amos and the Well-deserved End

WE ARE INQUIRING into the unique character of the prophetic word, trying to discover what it has to say to us today.

The Old Testament prophets fascinate us for two reasons. In the first place, the prophets' attention is quite firmly directed toward the future. They see sinister future events looming over the people of their own day. But the dangers of the future oppress us today, too, perhaps even more than they did in earlier generations. How does our view of the future compare with the prophetic one? Second, the prophets see the future as inextricably bound up with the present. This means that they move their own contemporary life into the glaring light of the future. The connection between present behavior and future destiny makes us uneasy, too. Can a dialogue with prophecy sharpen the criteria which determine the criticisms of our own time? It is for two reasons, then, that we ask: what is prophecy aiming at?

We direct our question first of all to the earliest example of a classical prophet in Israel—Amos of Tekoa. With Amos, we confront historical sources of the highest quality. Yet we must not expect a biography. For us, Amos's life is concealed in his preaching, a fact that is highly significant. Only in his words do we find something about his background and his profession. He comes from Tekoa, a village about eleven miles south of Jerusalem and six miles south of Bethlehem—a small military outpost belonging to the kingdom of Judah. There Amos had made a good living by raising sheep. Quite suddenly, we find him appearing as a prophet in the northern kingdom of Israel—certainly in the capital city of

Samaria, but also in Bethel, which was an important place of pilgrimage. This happened during a period of economic prosperity under Jeroboam II, around 760 B.C.

How is it that this man Amos came to be talking about the future and the present? In Amos's case, as in the case of all of the other Old Testament writing prophets, we have to exclude oracular techniques which were widespread in the ancient Near East: the interpretation of the stars, the examination of animals' entrails, the casting of lots, and so on. We also have to exclude any intoxicating, ecstatic condition of the mind in which the conscious self is blotted out. For autobiographical accounts have never come down to us from the ecstatics of the ancient Orient, but such accounts are not at all uncommon among Israel's classical prophets.

A favorite approach to finding an explanation for prophecy has been and still is trying to discover the impulse to prophetic speech in the prophet's critical analysis of his period, a criticism based on ancient Israel's divine law. But even this approach is not supported by the traditions which come to us from the classical prophets. The analysis of their own time, then, is not the basis of the prophetic preaching.

The Book of Amos gives a different answer to the question of why Amos began his public proclamation, and it gives this answer in three highly varying contexts.

We find the first part of the answer at the end of a rhetorical, didactic series of questions with which Amos defends his behavior to his skeptical listeners (3:8): "Since a lion has roared, who will not be afraid? Since the Lord has spoken, who will not prophecy?" This saying is a defense against the suspicion that Amos has come forth with his message of doom to Israel by his own initiative and in his own interests. He counters this criticism with a cogent proof, following the method used by teachers of wisdom of the time. Every event raises the question: what set it off? The sudden roaring of a lion makes a person tremble with fear; in the same way, Yahweh's address compels a person to pass the word on. Just as there is no way to avoid fearing a lion, there is also no possible way to remain silent when Yahweh's commission descends upon a person. With this argument, then, Amos energetically rejects the suspicion that he was talking on his own initiative or that he had sought a saying from Yahweh or that he had even extorted it by means of expert oracular procedures. The word of Yahweh came upon him even though he had not sought it at all. To his own alarm, he saw himself exposed to Yahweh's utterance, unwillingly but also inescapably. Resistance was impossible. Yahweh's word came as *verbum irresistibile*. It was not an inherited office that legitimated him, nor any social criticism on his own part. He was not motivated by any oracle he had sought for himself or by any Torah that had been passed on to him. It was a new word of Yahweh which overpowered him. The Lord has spoken. That is the only answer he gives when asked: why are you talking like this?

Amos undoubtedly means that he has been personally overcome with irresistible force by a new word. This emerges without any ambiguity at all from the other two textual complexes which legitimate his appearance.

The second textual complex (7:10-17) presents us with a scene which takes place at the sanctuary in Bethel. We have a contemporary reporter to thank for the account of this incident. The priest Amaziah, who is in charge of the sanctuary, sends a runner to tell King Jeroboam in Samaria, "Amos is instigating insurrection against you in the midst of the house of Israel; the land is no longer able to contain all his words. For thus Amos has said, 'Jeroboam shall die by the sword, and Israel shall depart into exile, away from its land.'" Thus Amos is denounced as an agitator who is working for a violent insurrection.

But the report keeps silent on two points of significance. It does not give the reasons which moved Amos to utter the threat of destruction—reasons which Amos himself continually stresses: Yahweh's word and Israel's injustice. And it does not say who is bringing about the catastrophe, for it is not Amos, as a conspirator, but the God of Israel himself, who brings all this to pass.

The priest knows very well what he has concealed. That is why he tries to save the man he has accused, before the king's decision can arrive: "Visionary, go! Flee away to the land of Judah! Eat bread there! For here is the royal sanctuary; here is the state temple." What kind of advice is this? It bursts with respect for both parties. Who is this Amaziah afraid of most, Jeroboam or Amos? Amaziah does not want to be partly responsible for the prophet's death, so he advises the doomed man to flee. He attempts the impossible. He wants to do right both by the king's prophetic judge (Amos) and by the prophet's kingly judge (Jeroboam) at the same time. By telling Amos to flee he wants to solve the predicament which is more his own than Amos's. Next to the distorted picture of the political revolutionary he places the picture of the religious eccentric; it is only possible to put up with him if he lets himself be controlled, and so protected, by the political order in force.

Amos shatters both of these caricatures with a sharp rejoinder: "I am no prophet, nor am I a prophet's disciple. I am rather a livestock breeder and one who slits mulberry figs." If we want to understand this seer, this is the most important negative conclusion we have to come to about him. He does not allow himself to be categorized as a professional political agitator. He is not urged on by any passion of his own or by the passion of any party. Least of all does he have to earn his bread as a professional prophet. He has a good income as a livestock breeder and, in addition, from the fig plantations he owns. It is worth noting how the first classical and canonical prophet stresses that he is a layman. He rejects the official term "prophet" when applied to himself. He does not want to be interpreted in terms of any sociological category or in the light of any general human need. He shatters Amaziah's "prophet" picture and many others at the same time. This preacher is in no way to be understood by probing his ego. He expressly denies three times the connection between his own self and what he proclaims: I—no prophet! I—no prophet's disciple! I—a livestock breeder! The last category completely covers his own personal needs.

But then how is Amaziah, the prototype of Amos's hearers, supposed to view him? Over against his threefold "I" in 7:14, Amos sets a threefold pointer to Yahweh in 7:15f.: "But *Yahweh* took me from following the flock, and *Yahweh* said to me: 'Go, prophesy unto my people Israel!' Now therefore hear the word of *Yahweh*!" These are sentences which open all of the curtains wide. Anyone who wants to understand Amos has to take Yahweh's compulsive grasp into account; he must see what Amos says as reflecting the invasion, the assault of Yahweh himself and his irresistible word. Amos can only be understood if we see him as a prophet in spite of himself. Alien though this notion may be for us today, it is an insight which we simply cannot avoid; any anthropological interpretation of this type of biblical prophet can only be one more in the series of political and psychological caricatures of the Amaziah type. From a scholarly or scientific point of view, however, the theological category is indispensible. The person who really wants to understand what is happening here has to face up to what is emphasized: "The Lord has spoken." He has spoken by fetching Amos personally away from his flocks. The Lord has spoken—this fact cuts him off from his ordinary everyday job, at least for a time. This sets him apart from other people and apart from all of the prophetic guilds. It turns him into someone unlike anyone else, a personality with a name of his own. This was his legitimation for resisting the reigning king and his official priests. The word of Yahweh, which he could not resist, made him irresistible even for Amaziah. Thus the upheaval of God's people, which the prophets led, was founded on an irresistible word.

But how are we supposed to conceive of this invasion of the irresistible word in concrete terms? Amos answers this himself in the third textual complex, which legitimates his behavior. It is the cycle of autobiographical visions of Amos 7:1–8; 8:1–2; 9:1–4. The insights we acquire here stir up the reader. The accounts are as taciturn as possible, yet precise in everything essential. We feel that the reporter is not motivated by any particular love of storytelling. Amos has been overpowered, and in his extremity he can only tell what is absolutely necessary. These brief sketches are crammed full of facts.

Each of them begins in the same way: "Thus the Lord Yahweh showed me." First of all, Amos has to look at a swarm of grasshoppers. They are stripping the whole country bare at a time when there is no more hope of a second harvest. This situation completely endangers the people's future. So Amos cries out,

"My Lord Yahweh, do forgive! How is Jacob to endure? For he is so small." Thereupon Yahweh withdraws this punishment; but then, in a new vision, Amos has to witness a rain of fire of unheard-of extent. It devours the great abyss, the endless waters from which all the springs and sources of the world are fed, so that the last fruitful acre is burned up by the flood of fire. Once again Amos cries out: "My Lord Yahweh, cease! How is Jacob to endure? For he is so small." In this cry of intercession no one can overlook Amos's solidarity with his people in their deadly danger. After this it is impossible to maintain that his acid words to Israel arise from his own desire for opposition. These first two visions clearly show a man who is profoundly affected, quite unexpectedly and most unwillingly, by God's will toward judgment. We see how vehemently Amos resists this divine will on behalf of the threatened people. And he does so in full, wakeful consciousness. This is the very opposite of an ecstatic absorption into the will of God. Yahweh's patience is once again shown in granting a reprieve on the basis of Amos's petition.

But then a third image strikes his eye. A plumb line is used to test a wall, to see if it is still straight and sturdy or if it ought to be pulled down. Now, for the first time, the vision is accompanied by Yahweh's voice: "Amos, what do you see?" In wakeful dialogue with his God, Amos has to learn to put into his own words what is revealed to him. He answers in startled monosyllables, "A plumb line." Then comes Yahweh's interpretation: "Hence I am setting a plumb line in the midst of my people Israel. I will no longer benignly pass them by." This third vision has more to say than the first two. It does not merely threaten disaster. Moreover, it shows that Yahweh's intervention is not determined by arbitrary motives. The motive is an incorruptible test, and it brings the judgment which Amos is no longer able to resist. The house of Israel is poised for destruction.

A fourth vision again compels Amos to put into his own words what he sees: a basket of ripe fruit, the token of harvest. The word *ḳájis* echoes the word *ḳēṣ*: the harvest is the end. So the test is now followed by the judgment: "The end has come for my people Israel. I will no longer benignly pass them by." The fifth vision shows that this is an end which no one will escape.

So Amos has been vanquished by Yahweh; he has been vanquished in a visionary dialogue which belongs to the psychic level of a heightened state of wakeful consciousness. A totally new word has been forced upon him concerning the end of Israel's history. Nothing can be explained here in the light of what happened to Amos against his own will. The decisions of his God have set him in complete isolation, decisions that have an inexorable power of conviction which Amos is incapable of escaping. Yet the content of what he learns is not at all otherworldly or transcendental. What happens to him is the very opposite of a mystical vision of God or a perception of higher worlds. Moreover, what has been transmitted to us about Amos frees us completely from any such misunderstanding. The word that is laid upon Amos applies in quite precise terms to the worldly, historical Israel in the days of Jeroboam and to its evil social and religious conditions. The sayings which he proclaims on the basis of his visions forcibly show this. This explains why Amos is able to captivate social reformers and revolutionaries.

But we only understand Amos as a prophet if we accept from him a reference which we cannot overlook, a reference that points back to Yahweh's assault, to what his God has revealed to him, to the conviction forced on him by Yahweh's words. Experiences of this kind are not for everyone. They were not for everyone in Amos's day, as Amaziah shows, and they are not for everyone today either. Modern men and women are confused because through the reference to God, something totally alien and incalculable enters into our history. But this must not make us fall victims to sociological leveling. It must not make us falsify Amos into the normal figure of a political analyst of his period or a social reformer or a utopian revolutionary. For us, perhaps nothing is more essential than a witness to the incomparable one who alone really ushers in the future.

We have met Amos as the witness to an irresistible word. He makes particularly evident what also applies basically to the other Old Testament prophets. Jeremiah can cry out in distress to his God, "Thou art stronger than I, and thou hast prevailed. I have become a laughingstock all the day; everyone mocks me" (Jer. 20:7 RVS). But the New Testament witnesses to Jesus

Christ come from an irresistible call, too. Acts 4:20 reports that Peter and John said, "We cannot but speak of what we have seen and heard." And Paul talks about the *anagkē*: "*Necessity* is laid upon me. Woe to me if I do not preach the gospel!" (1 Cor. 9:16).

This presents the church today and all of its responsible members with a question: Church, do you know—do your members know—that you owe your existence to a *verbum irresistibile*, to an irresistible word? Members, do you know that? Do we ask the prophets and apostles urgently enough what this word is? Do we not think far too much today about what we could just as well discuss in terms of psychological and sociological processes? We wrack our brains about what might be of interest for contemporaries. What can we offer as topics for discussion? We are on the lookout for variety, and at the end of it all we leave our contemporaries and ourselves alone with themselves and with ourselves. Instead of all that, what is really asked of us is to inquire about the one thing needful, the thing that was enjoined on the prophets and apostles by their Lord. It would seem that we are almost commanded vigorously to trim away the diversity from that which we offer in our efforts to please every taste. We must once again become aware of the way the Old and New Testament witnesses probe deeply into our world. The prophetic word, for example, became so important that it had literary-historical consequences, among other things. The collection of prophetic sayings as a literary genre has only existed since Amos. And this means that the irresistible word goes on working also as literature. *This* is how it wants us to read and accept it. It wants the reader to ask about the irresistible nature of its message, as a help toward the wholeness of life.

What do we find here that is so compelling? What is it that Amos finds impossible to be silent about? It is the absolute, fundamental certainty of *the end* of history as it has hitherto existed. This was burned into him by the fourth vision—the vision of the basket of ripe fruit. This was the terror of the roaring lion which shook Amos's life to its foundations. This is what Amaziah has found unendurable. And this is how Amos interpreted it: "Jeroboam shall die by the sword, and Israel shall depart into exile, away from its land."

For Amos and his people, this expulsion from their country is far more than just some historical misfortune. It means the cancellation of the gift of the land that had been made to them in the early period of their history; this gift was the seal of Yahweh's goodness and his election. So banishment from the land means the end of salvation history. In the cycle of sayings against the nations (Amos 1–6), Amos extends the word of judgment first of all to the Aramaeans and Philistines, the Ammonites and Moabites. Just as he calls to this hostile environment, so Yahweh cries to Israel in terms that shock and horrify: "I will not revoke it"—namely, the word about the end would stand.

The word about the end brings an indispensible key word into the biblical message. Amos stimulates us to think in radical and sober terms about the certainty of the end and to relate this certainty to many things which we, as a matter of course, think of as being permanent, as repeatable at will. Amos is able to stimulate our self-reflection when he varies his message about the end and gives it concrete form. He calls out the consequences to the priest Amaziah (7:17), "You yourself shall die on unclean land!" He threatens the women of Samaria (4:2f.), "You shall be hauled away with ropes and with harpoons . . . cast off toward Harmon." He uses assonance to claw at the minds of the pilgrims to Gilgal and Bethel—that Gilgal has to go into Gola (into exile) and Bethel (the house of God) will go to the devil. He peppers the word to Samaria's elite with irony. The men who are conscious that they are "the top people" in society and that they possess "top qualities" will be "at the top of the train of the deported." He picks up theological traditions, too, only to turn them upside down (3:2): "You only have I selected out of all the clans of the earth. Therefore I will requite upon you all your transgressions." Election must not be made a justification for self-complacency. It is a reason to fear judgment. Amos is able to show the end in radical form in many other ways too—in the form of a lament for the dead, in the form of an earthquake, or in the form of a warlike raid with hopeless panic. It is always the message of the end which the listener is inexorably forced to face up to.

If we look at the specific forms in which this is expressed, what strikes us in the midst of all the variations is a single constant: it is the "I" of Yahweh who brings about the end. "I will send a fire . . . , I will cut off . . . , I will slay" (1:4f., 7f.; 2:2f.); "I will turn my hand against them" (1:8); "I will punish" (3:2); "I will smite" (3:15); "I will pass through the midst of you" (5:17); "I will take you into exile" (5:27); "I abhor . . . , I hate . . . , I will deliver up (6:8); "I am setting a plumb line . . . , I will never again pass by them" (7:8; 8:2); "I will set my eyes upon them for evil and not for good" (9:4). So what brings about the end in all these different cases? Not Yahweh's absence; on the contrary, Yahweh's absence is the determining factor about the present. No, it is his undesired but inescapable coming. The people do not want it to happen, but they will not be able to stop him. That may be particularly important for us, in a life where God is often forgotten. What we have to think about is not the end as such, in all its different forms. What we have to consider is the unexpected prospect: to await the Incomparable Effective (God). So Amos 4:12 draws the conclusion, "Precisely because of what I am about to do to you, prepare to meet your God, Israel!" The message about the end is therefore exactly the same thing as the message about the inescapable encounter with God. In the tension between the present and the future, man sees too little if he only considers himself. The connection between present behavior and future destiny takes on a new dimension. The encounter with God, the Incomparable Effective, is the fundamental element of the irresistible word. It is an element which finds its new form in the New Testament word of the cross of Christ. It is the word about the end in which God's judgment is inescapably present.

But this only becomes fully comprehensible when we allow Amos to take us a considerable step further. Amos reiterated with great regularity in his sayings that the cause for the coming end was the injustice of the present. The coming end is a sin-caused end. Amos is definite about the future catastrophe; however, he does not think of the future in terms of danger, but rather in terms of guilt. In the end, the one whom men and women encounter is God, whose precepts they have forgotten. So the sober view of the end is above all a demand for self-examination. Amos's examples can stimulate us here.

Why does the war, which no one can resist, come about (2:13–16)? Because society treats unimportant little people with increasing contempt, to the point where a man and his father sleep with the same girl (2:6f.). A misuse of the relationships of dependence leads to an arbitrary infringement of the intimate sphere of young women. A dubious way of life like this leads to a far from dubious end. The reason for the coming misery is to be found in the present disregard of God's commandment to love and protect others.

Amos's critique goes far deeper than just measuring external obedience to the commandments as they have been proclaimed. No written commandment has forbidden people to lie on ivory beds, to lounge around on their couches, to bawl silly songs to the sound of the lute, or to drink wine straight out of the jugs. But if the style of life of the leading circles in Samaria is dominated by such actions, and if they are not "grieved over the ruin of Joseph," then these same leaders will lead the procession of the deported, too (6:1-7). Ought we consider at this point how our own leisure-time society relates to people and societies of the Third World?

Amos's criticism applies not least to religious festivities with their offerings and their hymns of praise (5:21-24). He condemns these as pleasurable self-indulgence and as attempts to gain religious merit. But Israel's God does not want to be the recipient of meritorious performances. His people are to receive from him. And what they are to receive is justice and righteousness. He will not allow himself to be degraded to the passive status of someone celebrated by others. He wants to remain what he has always been: the active one who gives his people the living waters of a just life and leads them toward a better righteousness. The worship service can never be self service. But that is what is happening here. God's leadership has been forgotten. "Hence I will lead you into exile beyond Damascus" (5:27).

The end is a deserved end, an end brought about by guilt. The word about guilt is the justification for the irresistible word about the end. If, according to Amos, the end leads with absolute certainty to an encounter with God in the future, the prophetic criticism of the present is dominated with equal certainty by the

God of Israel's unambiguous will. This link between the present and the future exists in God. In the individual case it can undoubtedly correspond to an immanent causality which is open to examination by reason. But this does not have to be the case. Present and future are more compulsively linked—indeed inextricably so—by the fact that God's people meet the same God in both present and future alike: here in commandment, there in judgment. Amos has two things to say about this: (1) the guilt of the present cannot be refused, and (2) the judgment of the future cannot be escaped. But by establishing this very fact, he is sinking the pilings for the bridge that leads over to the New Testament. For in the New Testament both statements are presupposed. Without them it is impossible to understand that Jesus Christ should take on himself the guilt we cannot contest and the judgment we cannot by ourselves escape.

But what is new in the New Testament is the third thing: in the midst of the end that we bring upon ourselves, a new life dawns through the intervention of Jesus Christ. The Book of Amos already suggests that new acts on God's part are to be expected on the other side of judgment. The ruined booth of David is to be rebuilt (9:11f.). The devastation, the degeneration, and the dispersion are not the last thing; they are only penultimate. God's power and grace will grant fruitfulness and peace, and with it a completely new homeland (9:11–15). Unconditional words of hope like these have raised Israel's eyes in the centuries that followed Amos, and have kept them wakeful in expectation of God's new acts.

At least one of the words of Amos himself points beyond the sin-caused end (5:4f.): "Thus Yahweh has said concerning the house of Israel: Seek me! Then you shall live. Do not seek Bethel! Do not enter into Gilgal! For Gilgal will surely depart into exile, and Bethel will become adversity." For Amos's contemporaries, to seek Yahweh and to seek the sanctuary were one and the same thing. This identification gives way to a clear antithesis. For the pilgrimages had become a camouflage for selfishness and contempt of other people. Bethel and Gilgal will therefore collapse in the end that the people have brought upon themselves. Life is to be found only with Israel's God. "Seek me! Then you shall live." *Post Christum crucifixum et resurrectum*, we can hear this call of Amos as an invitation to new life. Yet this call is and remains closely bound up with the message of the deserved end. Let me sum up how, in the light of the New Testament, Amos 5:4 emphasizes Amos's three essential statements.

1. Be absolutely certain that an end has been appointed for all evil! Nothing shady can last. Reckon with the fact that all injustice, all greed, and all scorn for other people have only death as their future. Can we see that this message about the coming end is also a blessing even now? For the people who commit evil and for the people who have to endure it, but also for the mass of the half-hearted, it is already the reverse side of the Gospel. "Seek me! *Then* you shall live!"

2. Realize that we have brought the threatened end on ourselves! With this accusation, Amos helps us recognize our own involvement in this life which is so often marred by failure. Above all, he opens our eyes to see that in the end, which we have deserved, we shall meet God himself. But under the cross of Christ we experience that no end can ever separate us from the love of God—no kind of trouble, not even death. "Seek me! Then you shall *live!*"

3. It is in this light that we can travel the road from the present into the future as reconciled ones, as acquitted felons, those given amnesty from prosecution. We now understand God's exhortation through Amos—"Seek me! Then you *shall* live!"—in a new way, as an invitation to the discipleship of Jesus. We are permitted to set foot afresh every day on the bridge that leads to the future—in unequivocal admission of guilt, in unambiguous concern for righteousness, and in unconditional readiness for reconciliation. "Seek *me!* Then you *shall live!*"

For we have learned that resistance against the irresistible word is vain. It is as vain for us later hearers of that word as it once was for Amos. Irresistible!

2

THE EFFECTIVE WORD

*Hosea and the
Healing of the
Incorrigible*

IN THE MIDDLE of a violent dispute, the prophet Hosea cries out, as an utterance of his God's will, "I strike by prophets, slay them by words of my mouth. My justice then breaks forth like light" (6:5). According to this the prophets are to be experienced as effective instruments through whom God wields a decisive blow. With the prophets he chops down everything that is wrong. Indeed the prophet is the weapon of death, clearing out of the way whatever blocks the path of justice: "My justice then breaks forth like light." Now whoever looks at Hosea's words more closely can feel the actual swinging of the sword through the written transmission of the text. Hosea sees himself torn hither and thither by his God's passions—torn between merciless darkness and luminous intimacy, between wrath and love, between disappointment and hope. In this strange back-and-forth, we can discover in Hosea how his God's word shows itself to be an active word. It is the effective word. But two questions need to be answered. How does that word work, and what does it effect?

The first chapters of the Book of Hosea initially withhold an answer to these questions. Before the question about public efficacy is raised at all, Chapters 1 and 3 go into the question of the prophet's personal preparation. His God's effective word will first of all become a reality in the prophet's private life. We therefore have to ask at the start: how is the prophet equipped to be an effective tool?

Chapters 1 and 3 tell us about three unprecedented impositions. At first there is no question here of militant blows. We are instead brought into the sphere of intimacy. Yet the marriage scenes are related to the public commission. The personal demands become symbolic acts.

Let us look at the first of them. It is explicitly introduced (1:2) as "the beginning of what Yahweh said through Hosea: 'Go, take for yourself a wife of whoredom and children of whoredom!'" So God's speech *through* Hosea begins with a speech *to* Hosea. This special charge to Hosea is singular enough. But the question of personal obedience is one that every messenger is faced with. And unusual though the demand to Hosea is, there is no doubt that public messengers always have to reckon with exceptional impositions. Are we perhaps all too deaf to this fact in our times of plenty?

Hosea is to take a *whore* as his wife. There is hardly any other sphere in which humans are so super-sensitive as when they are choosing a companion for life. Anyone who dares to interfere has to watch his step! But here the unthinkable is demanded: to marry a prostitute—a slut who is highly unsuited for marriage, indeed repugnant. (Just think for a moment what congregations expect of their pastor's wives!) But it is questionable whether Hosea is being asked to enter into marriage with some random tart who has thrown herself at the head of goodness knows whom for money. Probably it is not a streetwalker that is meant here. In eighth-century Israel, we ought rather to think of the intrusion of Canaanite fertility rites. In these rites women sat themselves down in the sacred groves and waited for strangers to come and have intercourse with them. But for Hosea, these cultic bridal rites especially are nothing but whoredom. For they are a document of unfaithfulness toward the love of Israel's God. And yet it is precisely this that Hosea is supposed to act out with his marriage: "For the land goes a-whoring away from Yahweh" (1:2b). He has to consummate and to demonstrate his God's utter disappointment. Yahweh's beloved, his wife Israel, runs away from him in order to give herself to an untold number of foreigners who represent the false gods. Hosea is to put into living terms, in his own existence, Yahweh's ache and Israel's guilt.

The second challenge is no less upsetting. It too intervenes in one of the most sensitive events of a marriage; it involves the naming of children. Even today this action of naming children provides an opportunity to express one's own most personal experiences and longings, love and gratitude, joy and hope. But Hosea is expected to give his three children names which are not normally personal names at all, and which indeed are gruesomely repellent because of their meaning. The eldest son must be called Jezreel. "Jezreel"—that is the name of a city and a district. In this context, the name of the city is clearly reminiscent of a bloodbath perpetrated by the ruling dynasty of Jehu. As the name for a child, Jezreel is as monstrous a name as if we in Germany were to burden a son of ours with the name "Auschwitz" or Americans were to burden a son of theirs with the name "Hiroshima." Through his name, Hosea's first child is to be a continual reminder that Yahweh will requite the blood-guiltiness of Jezreel. The second child, a little daughter, is to be given the name "Without Mercy." That sounds as shocking as if we were to call a child "Hopeless" instead of "Hope." The third name is evidence of the complete breach between Israel and God, for this child is to be called "Not My People." It is as if we were to choose "I Hate You" for a little boy instead of "Matthew," or "Devil" instead of "Daniel." We notice that all three names shock the hearer into listening to what is being said. When Hosea is forced to intertwine his threatening words so closely with his family life, it is a continual, sinister reminder of his message of doom.

At a later time in his life the third challenge comes—an imposition of a quite different kind. In 3:1 it reads: "Go once again, love a woman who loves a friend and practices adultery—as Yahweh loves the children of Israel, although they turn to other gods and love cakes of raisins." This may have been the same woman who had borne him the three children. The only thing she has been faithful to is her unfaithfulness; she has once again gone with other men. Now Hosea is supposed to take her back again; he is to document through a new symbolic act that in spite of everything it is not his final intention to reject her—even though the law strictly forbids anyone to take back a divorced person (Deut. 24:1ff.). Yahweh in his love never stops loving the Israelites, although in their self-deception they promise themselves a pleasanter existence with other gods; so, in the same way, in this new symbolic act Hosea is to pay a heavy price in order to win back the straying adulteress: "fifteen shekels of silver and a lot of barley" (3:2). (In cash alone he would not be able to come up with the money!) He has to offer all this to the woman's last lover in order to get her back legally. So in his actions, Hosea not only becomes a pattern for Israel's guilt and a pattern for God's wrath, he also represents God's solicitous, wooing love as well. What his God demands of him always penetrates deeply into his private life, into his most intimate sphere. He is expected to do what is utterly alien to him—indeed repellent—in order to strip the reality of the situation bare. He is expected to do what strikes a permanently and conspicuously jarring note, which raises questions; and finally, he has to do what he has to pay dearly for. To be called into the service of the God of Israel is not a paying proposition, not like a lucrative business venture. It costs the messenger a great deal in every respect. But it is a word of this kind, more than any other, which continues to be heard through the millenia as God's word.

The love-marriage-harlotry theme goes on working in Hosea's whole proclamation. Whatever he is talking about—religious practice or economics or politics—he speaks about Yahweh as the loving and spurned husband and about Israel as the faithless wife. We have no evidence that the marriage symbolism was used for Yahweh and Israel before the time of Hosea. Did it merely originate in his rhetorical skill? We have seen that it was forced on him as a way of interpreting and remolding reality. Viewed in the context of the history of ideas, what is at the back of this is an intensive discussion with contemporary Canaanite mythology— a discussion that was pregnant with consequences. It is an exciting process of adoption and polemic. For by choosing the parable of marriage, Hosea for the first time risks taking over the mythical concept of a divine marriage.

According to the Baal-myth, the rain is the sperm, so to speak, with which the god fertilizes the divine Woman and Mother Earth, so that she is able to bring forth her vegetation. This mythical viewpoint can be seen in many different forms in the vegetation religions of Israel's environment. It is linked with cults like the "sacred marriage" between the king and the queen, between priests and priestesses. By means of sympathetic magic, these marriages are designed to guarantee the fruitfulness of the soil as well as of the animal and human world. Widespread sexual rites were then the result—rites like the ones we have indicated, for example, in which young women (and older ones, too) were involved in the sacred groves of Canaanite cultic practice. The clearest evidence of these practices has come down to us from Herodotus. Some of Hosea's statements are only comprehensible in this light—for example, 4:13f.: ". . . under oak and terebinth, because their shade is so pleasant; there your daughters play the whore. . . . The priests go aside with whores. . . ." So what Hosea calls "playing the whore" does not mean only a reckless giving way to lust and passion, a sowing of one's wild oats in unrestrained lust. In Canaan it had a ritual character as well and was therefore religiously legalized, so to speak. There seem to have been proofs of participation in the bridal initiation rites which evidently took the form of scratches or cuts, or fillets bound around the forehead, necklets with pendants, and so forth. That is what is behind 2:2: "Let her remove the marks of her prostitution from her face, and the signs of her adultery from between her breasts!" The children who were conceived in the sacred grove had to be sacrificed to the deity in whose sphere of influence their conception had taken place. That is the background of the Canaanite sacrifice of the firstborn, which Israel rejected. Here Hosea subjects the practice to savage irony (13:2): "Those who sacrifice men kiss calves," meaning the images of the sacred calves used in the vegetation cults. We do not know how widely the Canaanite influence had penetrated Israel between the days of Elijah and Hosea's time. Probably it was considered progressive to take over some of the practices we have described. Israelite circles who clung to the old ways were no doubt told that after all Yahweh was a desert God, and that in the cultivated lands the ancient Canaanite fertility ritual with its mythical and cultic experience was to be preferred as the science appropriate to the place. Modernism and greediness go hand in hand.

At this point Hosea's criticism intervenes in Yahweh's name (2:8): "She [the unfaithful wife] does not know that I gave her the grain, the new wine, and the olive oil, that I lavished upon her silver and gold." What is happening here? Hosea is stressing first of all that the God of the desert, Yahweh, is the God of the cultivated lands as well—he and he alone. All the fruits and treasures of the earth come from him: "I am Yahweh your God from the land of Egypt. You know no God but me, there is no savior besides me" (13:4). Second, in Hosea the mythical marriage between the heavenly Baal and Mother Earth turns into the bond between Yahweh and Israel—a bond based on law and on love. The sexual components recede entirely. Yahweh alone causes fertility. He has a bond with Israel. Third, the sexual rites which were a part of Canaanite life are condemned as whoredom, as being nothing more than prostitution. They are a betrayal of Yahweh and a defection to Canaan's Baals. "They fornicate but do not increase," says Hosea (4:10). They are quite simply incapable of fulfilling life. It is in this way that Hosea's adoption of the Canaanite cult is a polemical one. For in this way he transforms the myth of the divine marriage into the call for a return home to Israel's first husband. This is the way he clarifies unambiguously the old creed in his discussion with the spirit of his own day. The call to a bond of love with the universal Creator of all things confronts a religion which offers a mythical explanation of the world and a cultic increase of production and of lust.

The Yahweh parable of the loving-and-later-left husband therefore serves the conflict with a modernism in Israel which considered itself to be progressive. What was at stake was far more than a decorative, pictorial manner of speaking.

The other Yahweh parables are also far more than linguistic adornments. Hosea offers them in a variety which we meet with nowhere else. Apart from the images of the husband, the father, and the physician—we shall come to these later—we have the picture of the hunter. According to 7:12, Israel has lost her political bearings and is running about helplessly, hither and thither, turning now to Egypt, now to Assyria. Then Yahweh throws his net over her, as if she were a fluttering bird, throws his dart at her, and brings her down. Hosea does not shrink back from theriomorphic images. In 5:14, Yahweh says, "I am like a lion to Ephraim, like a young lion to the house of Judah; I, even

I, will rend and go away, I will carry off, so that none shall rescue." Everyday language is simply inadequate to bring Israel to confront the wrath of Yahweh. So he cries in 13:7f., "I become like the lion to them, like the panther I will lurk along the way. I will attack them like a she-bear who is robbed of her young, and tear open the enclosure of their heart" (he means the chest). With images like these the fear of Yahweh himself assails the listeners. Hosea 5:12 sounds outrageous, almost blasphemous: "I am like pus to Ephraim, like rottenness to the house of Judah." This is the way Yahweh talks when his wounded people turn to the mighty king of Assyria; powerful though he is, he is a helpless physician, a quack when Yahweh himself spreads through Israel's body like pus from a festering sore and putrifying gangrene. No one had ever dared to talk about Yahweh like this before.

The passion of Yahweh's anger drags the prophet into the heat of his emotions. Pious traditions and aesthetic tastes have to recede behind the will to proclaim Yahweh's terrible and irresistible sovereignty and efficacy. But in the surge of passion, the other side must not be forgotten either. Where the word of salvation is possible, even at a late stage, there Yahweh's voice uplifts and refreshes his people: "I will be as dew to Israel" (14:5) or even "like a luxuriant juniper" (14:8), a proper fruit tree. Here Hosea is not afraid of any similarity to the language of the vegetation cults. For out of his free power and ardent love Yahweh can give all the things that the Baals have in any case no disposal over. Most of the Yahweh parables appear in "I am" sayings. Israel is continually to perceive that it is Yahweh himself who desires to confront her, whatever form he may assume.

If the Yahweh parables have let us feel *how* the prophetic commission achieves its effect with the power of the word, we must now ask, *what* is it that Yahweh wants to achieve through Hosea's word? What is his aim in his passionate surge of anger and love? I think that we are bound to extract a single, clear answer out of all the variation in his sayings. What God wants of his people is for them to return to their first love.

There are good reasons why the tone and content of the individual sayings differ so widely. They are gathered from twenty-five years of turbulent history between about 750 and 725 B.C.

The situations of Hosea's listeners change. Their reactions require new answers. And the love which wrestles to regain the first love remains inventive: it strives toward its goal through alienation and through exposure. The place where the listener is sought out is in the forlorn existence with the false lover. There the gifts of creation are turned into idols, and what ought to be merely the penultimate thing becomes the ultimate one. Greed becomes suicidal, readiness for seduction grows into self-dissipation, the one who has been liberated will not follow the liberator, and so the Creator of all things is undiscoverable. The place where a listener to Hosea's word stands must emerge in any given case. And it must emerge with methods by which he can be persuaded to return to his first love. I shall start by mentioning some typical attempts, which still retain their permanent importance. Then we shall turn our attention in more detail to the fundamentals of what is ultimately the decisive thing.

1. In one of the earliest sayings, Hosea calls out in Yahweh's name (2:2): "Accuse your mother! Accuse her! For she is not my wife, and I am not her husband any longer." Here Israel's sons—a group which is not defined any more closely than that—are mobilized against their mother. Youth is to oppose the establishment; individuals with insight are to state quite clearly what damage is being caused by an infatuated majority. The concept of collective thinking is blown apart in a remarkable way. So the God of the Bible links hope for every generation with groups of clear-eyed sons who listen to him afresh and who are then prepared to say what they have heard.

2. We find a second attempt in the continuation of this passage. The accusers are to offer a warning, or rather an ultimatum (2:2f.): "Let her remove the marks of her prostitution . . . lest I strip her naked . . . I will make her like a wilderness . . . and let her die of thirst." What is demanded secondly, therefore, is a decisive departure from seductive activities and from foolish hopes. The clarity is salutary, and segregation can be helpful. But Hosea complains that in his time both attempts fail. The sons, like their mother, continue to run after false lovers; they are in the thrall of passion (2:4f.).

3. The third attempt to win back the runaway is a treatment

for the addiction itself, a cure by deprivation (2:6f.): "I will now hedge up her way with thorns . . . so that she cannot find her paths. . . . Then she shall seek them, but not find them. . . . Then she shall say, 'I will set out and return to my first husband, for then it was better for me than now.'" What the warning through the word was incapable of doing is now achieved by a reformatory measure blockading the access to temptation. Many a person confirms gratefully that this has been a protection in the hour of temptation—that the path was blocked.

4. But how long does this return to the first love last? In 6:4, after a song of repentance on Israel's part, we hear Yahweh struggling with himself: "What shall I do for you, O Ephraim? What shall I do to you, O Judah? Your loyalty is like morning mist, like dew that vanishes early." All the good intentions have vanished as quickly as the ground mist is dissipated on a summer morning, as swiftly as the early dew disappears before the sun. Hosea's God does not deceive himself about the instability of the will to return. And who is not in a position to confirm this? So most of Hosea's sayings end in profound somberness. The judgment of doom is inexorable. Despairingly, Yahweh declares: "She did not know that I gave her" all she needed, "but she forgot me, says Yahweh" (2:8, 13) Israel ends up lost, with her false lovers.

5. But even when the unfaithful beloved forgets Yahweh, Yahweh still cannot leave her. In 2:14f. we read: "I myself will now allure. I will bring her into the wilderness." Is not this judgment? Yes, the wilderness, the desert, means total privation. But what else does Yahweh do in this zero-point situation? "I woo her heart. Then I will give her from there her vineyards. . . . There she shall willingly follow as in the days of her youth, as at the time when she came out of the land of Egypt." In the wilderness above all, where there are no longer any enticing voices, the heart is open for the wooing of love; and the beloved follows her lover once more.

Right down to this final word we feel the ever new, ever varying endeavors to win back to a fulfilled life the beloved who has been enticed away and deceived. But Hosea's most extreme efforts are still ahead of us.

There are two sayings of the most profound hopelessness in Hosea which perhaps only the person who has failed in the face of temptation's overwhelming power can understand—failed in spite of all the good examples, warnings, barriers, and new beginnings. The first of these sayings is in 5:4: "Their deeds do not permit them to return to their God. For a spirit of whoredom is at work in their midst, so that they do not know Yahweh." Hosea knows how pregnant with consequences the first lapse is. It is such a terribly short step from the first experiment with the idol to addictive dependence on it, and then to complete forgetfulness of God. The succession of acts increasingly winds its chains round our feet. That is what another saying means when it points out (7:2): "Now their deeds encircle them, they occur before my face." So Hosea sees his hearers as completely hemmed in without freedom to move, ringed round as if they were in a besieged fortress, and unable to repent even with the best of their intentions. Some of us may know what this terrible enchainment means. Or should I perhaps say, which of us does not know what it means?

But it is at this very point that for me the essential thing about Hosea's effectiveness begins—that is, his word for the utterly hopeless, for the people who despair of God and the world and themselves.

Let us turn to Hosea 11 and begin with verse 8. The Lord says, "How shall I surrender you, O Ephraim? Give you up, O Israel? How can I surrender you like Admah? Treat you like Zeboiim?" —that is to say, destroy you utterly like Sodom and Gomorrah. These questions end the great accusation discourse in 11:1-7. There Yahweh as Father takes legal proceedings against Israel, his son. Israel's whole life shows obstinate recalcitrance. The guilt is doubly heavy. For one thing, in every phase the good deeds of the Father were met by an evil reaction on Israel's part. For another, the series of rebellious acts is continuous, uninterrupted. At the end of the long history of God's demonstrations of love and his severity, we are told, "They have refused to return to me" (11:5b) and "my people are bent on turning away from me" (11:7a). According to the law about the stubborn and rebellious son in Deut. 21:21, only the death penalty was possible for such a son. But just at this very point God's struggle with himself begins: "How shall I surrender you? Give you up?" It is the cry of the Father's heart which is bleeding away, torn between law and love. Love has from the very beginning determined Yahweh's ways with his son. "When Israel was young, I loved him. . . . I drew them with ropes of love" (11:1, 4). But Israel's answer was always to turn away. What now? What is to have the final say? Out of these questions we hear Yahweh's admonition to himself: How can I let my love slip away? This is the point when, following the accusation, the punishment must be pronounced. Instead of that, the Father admonishes himself. He goes on: "I will not execute my burning anger. I will not again destroy Ephraim" (11:9a). Yahweh had already wielded the sword in Israel's cities (11:6a) as an educational measure in the hope that Israel would repent. Now the judge decides that at the end, love shall be the final word. It is on this personal decision by God that the future of the listener is founded. His future does not depend on the faulty human decision between repentance and estrangement. The coexistence between God's wrath and his love has an end too. Verse 8b says explicitly: "My heart turns against me, my remorse burns intensely." God implements in himself the repentance which man refuses to implement. The Hebrew expression *hapak* is even a reminder of the annihilating overthrow with which judgment fell on Sodom and Gomorrah (Gen. 19:25, and correspondingly on Admah and Zeboiim, Deut. 29:22). This judgment now takes place within God's own self, as it were. He overthrows his own anger. (Here it is impossible to avoid thinking of the cross of Christ as the seal of this message of Hosea's.) The parallel statement to the reference to the overthrow says in 11:8b: "My remorse burns intensely." God is stirred up and dominated by his remorse. Here we cannot overlook or ignore the key word "passion."

Passion of this kind sounds very human, especially in relation to the struggle between anger and love, justice according to the law and free pardon, and acquittal of the guilty. This very humanity, together with the victory of love, belongs to the essence of God's deity. The textual context brings this out—especially as the reason for the renunciation of punishment—when it goes on in 11:9b: "For I am God and not a man, the Holy One in your midst, and I will not become enraged." Just because God calls himself in question, just because he overthrows his wrath and not the guilty son, he remains true to himself, letting love have the last word.

In 14:4 this astonishing process described in Hosea 11 is reduced to the precise and clear-cut concept of spontaneous love, love proceeding from free will. Here Hosea moves (very significantly) from the picture of the father and the judge to the image of the physician: "I will heal their apostasy. I will love them spontaneously." The apostasy from which the obstinate son no longer wished to or could turn aside is now treated and healed like a severe illness. The medicine of love comes solely from God's own will. Its premise is not man's repentance. On the contrary, this love applies above all to the binding incapacity for repentance which Hosea referred to in 5:4 and 7:2. So Hosea announces a physician for the people, who are in themselves without hope.

The people's encirclement by wickedness and their incapacity to do better is now ushered into a spring of love and hope. Following 14:5, Hosea illuminates this in a passage of extreme beauty (14:6–8), full of unusual images that go to the utmost of sensuous loveliness. Here a wealth of love-song motifs is brought together. Otherwise we meet them only in Solomon's "Song of Songs." These love-song motifs are no doubt part of this physician's therapy. Verse 5 states, "I will be as dew to Israel; he shall flower like a lily." In the Song of Solomon the lily is used seven times as an image for the beloved (2:1, 16, passim) and dew for the wonderful freshness of love. "Fragrance like the forest of Lebanon" and the comparison with wine (Hos. 14:6–8) belong to the Song of Solomon too. "Your love is more fragrant than wine," sings the Song of Solomon in 4:10. We read in Hosea 14:7, "They shall again dwell in my shadow," a phrase which corresponds to the Song of Sol. 2:3, where the most delightful place in the world is "to sit in the shadow of my beloved." So the key word about spontaneous love in 14:4 is developed in a way that must have uplifted and brought joy to its contemporaries. Once again, the language of the prophet is put at the service of the glowing passion of his God. It means that his readers enter into the climate and atmosphere, even into the fragrance, of healthy life and intimate love with all the freshness and power of the senses, with dew and flowers, with wine, and with the scent of the cedars of Lebanon.

Must we at the end point out that this God, who wrestles or fights for those who are his, is a very different God from the God of the philosophers, the unmoved Mover, and the First Cause? Or that he is a very different God, too, from the enforcer of the law who we find discussed by some later Jews and Calvinists when they followed neither Hosea nor the Pauline epistles? Hosea's winning back of the adulteress in 3:1 and the judgment passed on the incorrigibly obstinate son in 11:5f. has shown that this God can do what the law says is impossible (Deut. 21:18ff.; 24:1ff.): the obstinate son and the faithless wife experience a wholly new, unconditional, and final love and sit in the shadow of the beloved. Hosea's prophecy points in the direction of Pauline insights: "God has done what the law, weakened by the flesh, could not do" (Rom. 8:3). The divine wrestling and suffering which we find in Hosea was sealed in Jesus Christ. In Jesus, God fulfilled the repentance which his people failed to fulfill. In Jesus, God took the judgment on himself instead of enforcing it on them. In Jesus, love was victorious over wrath. The judge has become a physician; the physician has become a sweetheart.

May a breath of this passion move all of us in our endangered world! For the world is endangered only through our failure to return to the first love. In praying for the breath of the Spirit, we must be completely clear about the fact that God's passion quite unequivocally desires compassion and the love that is undeserved.

And one more therapeutic hint for Christians, for Jews, and for those without hope: It is only under the continuing effect of the prophetic and apostolic word that, even in all adversities, we can keep the most pleasant place in the world "to sit in the shadow of the beloved."

3

THE UNMASKING WORD

Micah and the Pious Leadership Circles

PROPHECY IS ESSENTIALLY a ministry of disclosure, a stripping bare. Israel's great prophets do not merely lift the veil of the future in order to destroy false expectations; at the same time, they expose the conduct of their contemporaries. They do so in a way that brings into full view the secret motivations and concealed intentions behind what these people are doing. Prophets tear the masks away and show the true face of the people behind them. Among these kinds of prophets, Micah is one of the greatest in his penetration of the camouflage. He sees two groups of people as being most intensively concerned with the art of masquerading: the political authorities and the public representatives of religion and piety.

We can learn from Micah what the task of unmasking is. It is a task that is urgently needed, and yet very difficult. It is one of the indispensable duties of the church, its ministers, and its members. Micah can be particularly eye-opening about those who seek power and those who possess power. But that is only half the task. We shall see that Micah practices unmasking with particular concentration when he is dealing with the religious authorities. So the church, too, must allow what Micah did to be enforced on itself first of all. All the things that are concealed behind ecclesiastical walls, the clergy's sacred vestments, and beneath the worshiper's sacred smiles must be brought to light. As members of Christ's body, Christians will have to wage war against their own hypocrisy before anything else. Micah will help us to practice this struggle so that we can continue to wage it for

the benefit of the world around us. To help us understand Micah
better, let me clarify two preliminary questions at the outset.

1. What function did Micah have in his own environment?
The discovery we start with from here is a negative one. Curi-
ously enough, in the writings that have been passed down to us,
Micah is never called a "prophet." The name Micah(el) is one of
the most common personal names. Ever since the excavations of
the ancient north Syrian royal city of Ebla (tell mardikh)—the
texts are from the twenty-third century B.C.—we have known
that this name has been in active use for more than four millenia,
down to the present day. Our Micah was distinguished from
many others of the same name by the addition of his home town:
Micah of Moresheth. That is what he is called in the opening of
the Book of Micah, in 1:1; but this is also what he is called a hundred years later by the "elders of the land" in Jer. 26:17ff. There
they quote his saying about the downfall of Jerusalem; they quote
it in defense of Jeremiah, who was supposed to be condemned to
death because of a similar threat. So Micah was known to the
elders of Judah as Micah of Moresheth. There is some evidence
to suggest that he himself belonged to this circle of the "elders of
the land" as the representative of his home town.

As elder of Moresheth, Micah would have belonged to the
group of men who had to maintain the law at the town gate when
there were disputes or when a misdemeanor or crime had been
committed. In the most important statement he makes about
himself (3:8), he describes his life's duty like this: "But as for me,
I am full of authority, justice, and courage, to declare to Jacob his
rebelliousness and to Israel his delinquency." So his authority
and fearlessness serve "justice." This makes him a direct rival to
those public officials in Jerusalem about whom he declares in
3:1, 9 that their duty was to further "justice." "Is it not your
responsibility to foster justice?" So the foundation of Micah's
prophetic office seems to be that awareness of justice which belonged to his duties as elder of Moresheth. At all events, he does
not want to lay claim to any special charismatic position in this
respect. He holds that other people too should be equally responsible for justice.

2. When we say that he belonged to Moresheth, what significance does this have? Moresheth lay in the Judean hills over twenty miles southwest of Jerusalem above the level of the coastal plain which ran along the Mediterranean Sea. There were five different places within a circumference of about six miles which were all fortified against the enemies who threatened the safety of the mountains of Judah and Jerusalem itself. In Micah's days these places were occupied by soldiers, officers, and commissioned officers who were in communication with the high command in Jerusalem. There was a lively traffic between Jerusalem and the Moresheth area. Archaeologists have found evidence for this in pottery shards of storage jars which were used for grain and other such commodities, and which bear the royal stamp (lmlk). As "the king's property" they point to the central military organization of Judah. Many examples of pottery with the king's seal were also found in Moresheth itself (tell ed-ǧudēde). Some of Micah's statements are easier to understand if we look for the ruling powers he attacks—among the officers and civil servants attached to these occupying forces. He often champions what he calls "my people," his own countrymen. As their elder, he probably feels especially responsible for them. He defends "his people's" women and children against the men who confiscate their houses and land; or he gives his support to "his people" in Jerusalem, by whom he means the husbands and fathers who have been pressed into forced labor there. Perhaps the military administration had arranged for them to be sent to Jerusalem.

This is roughly how we have to imagine the situation in which Micah tears away the masks which conceal the true faces of men. He always refers to quite specific happenings. These are not made the starting point for theories, but they lead to the tracing of similar proceedings. We find in Micah 2 and 3 four "model" examples of his unmasking procedure, two major and two minor cases, one probably from Moresheth and three certainly from Jerusalem.

What is happening in the first case? Micah's polemic is preserved for us in 2:1–11. It begins with accusations and threats against those in power who snatch houses and land for themselves

and carry husbands and sons into forced labor. Micah begins
with an exclamation, "Woe!" This was the cry used in the lament
for the dead in Israel. It is, as it were, the death sentence which
already rings in the ears of the accused (2:1f.): "Woe to those
who lie awake and plan evil upon their beds, so that when morning comes they may perform it, because it is in the power of their
hand. They covet fields and seize them, and houses and take them;
they oppress a man and his family, a man and his inheritance."
Micah is picking up one of the basic commandments of the divine
law (Lev. 19:13): "You shall not oppress your neighbor or rob
him." The cause of violent acts against persons and property,
Micah says, is "coveting," which is the only offense that is actually rejected twice in the Decalogue (Exod. 20:17a, b). Micah
traces this coveting back to dreams that go through the mind during sleepless nights and which quickly crystallize into wishes and
well-thought plans. These plans are dangerous because the plan-
ners have the power to carry them out. The more power a person
has, the more he must keep a check on what he plans to do, or the
more he needs a watchful prophet. Perhaps an officer must adapt
himself to be quartered in a garrison town for a long period of
time. Plans take shape quickly: to evacuate a house for himself
and to compel the residents to forced labor. Micah at once hurls
the Lord's plan against the plans of men (2:3): "Therefore thus
says the Lord: Behold, I am planning disaster." Man's evil planning has already been encircled by God's superior plan. Micah
becomes more precise: "You will not remove your necks from
disaster; you will no longer be able to walk erect!" Micah even
puts into their mouths a dirge for them to sing: "We are utterly
ruined. Our captors divide our field!" Expropriation and expulsion threaten the expropriators and expellers. They fall into the
pit they had dug for others. That is what Micah had to say.

   Immediately the indignation of those who have been attacked
is aroused. They react sharply with two sets of three short sentences. The first three (2:6), with their three negatives, adopt the
pose of the official religious superintendent: "Do not preach!"
—thus they preach—"one should not preach of such things; dis-
grace will not overtake us." People who can have their way with
the small-time farmers think they can surely be able to cope with

the prophet and his rabble-rousers. How can anyone reproach them with their nightly reflections and their military measures, equipped as they are with authority from Jerusalem itself? How can anyone deny that they walk uprightly? How can anyone threaten them with expulsion from the country? Real estate and the working man's rights are not subject for sermons. This is the mask of the spiritual superintendents.

With the second set of three sentences they play the part of being the protectors of the one true faith (2:7a). These sentences are questions, formulated as if for a cross-examination: "Is then the house of Jacob accursed? Can it be said that the Lord is impatient? Are his acts of this kind?" This mask radiates the complacent confidence of faith. There is a reminiscence of the psalms: "The Lord is slow to anger and abounding in steadfast love" (Ps. 86:15). God's deeds are confessed in the words of Israel's creed: out of Egypt, through the wilderness, into this promised land—these are God's authentic, established acts. How can Micah threaten eviction from the country? These people are confident of blessing. Are they not right?

Micah answers, "Yes, my words also do good to those who walk uprightly" (2:7b). Micah by no means intends to minimize God's goodness. His goodness is valid for all who adjust their lives accordingly and let themselves be liberated by it throughout their lives. "But you rise against my people as an enemy!" (2:8a). The declaimed confidence in salvation seems devout, but it is pure egotism. They actually minimize God's goodness. They are taking God's gift of the land for themselves, but are denying it to the small farmers. Now Micah exposes the real complexion of the people who have power. He points to four cases which provide the evidence for his accusation of violence toward people and property. In the first case (2:8), peace-loving pedestrians are being robbed of their clothes. The holdups, carried out by plundering soldiers from one or another of the barracks, are evidently well known. In case two (2:9a), women are being driven out of their own houses. Perhaps these are women who have been left alone because their husbands have been carried off to forced labor. They are being "driven out" as if by a foreign occupying power. Case three (2:9b), shows that even children are the victims of greed. Perhaps the ancient text is thinking of the place of sleep which they are robbed of when their mother loses her house. In case four (2:10), the defendants enforce the law of distraint or seizure far too rigorously. For the slightest trifle the heaviest burdens are being laid on little, unimportant people; perhaps they are actually enslaved because of their debts. At all events they have to suffer humiliating and painful penalties. After incidents like these Micah can only toss back the question to the hypocrites: "Is then Jacob's house accursed? Is Yahweh impatient? Are his acts of this kind?" This is how Micah tears away the masks from the alleged guardians of the true faith. He does not do it by means of a monologue, a lecture. He uses dialogue, indeed a violent debate, in argumentative defense of what he has been charged to say and in a specific refutation of the objections. Without the dispute it is hardly possible to penetrate the zone of hypocrisy.

The dispute does not end without Micah's drawing of contrasting picture to the prophetic office to which he knows himself to be called. He etches in the contrast with a biting brand of humor (2:11): "If a man were to go about uttering wind and lies, saying, 'I preach to you of wine and whiskey,' he would be a proper preacher for this people." This portrait of a superstar preacher shows the naked face of his opponents in all its unvarnished truth. The real deep-down motivation behind their actions is nothing but private self-indulgence. The prophet who is after their own hearts can preach empty nothings and mouth petty nonsense without any interference. He may even make interesting what is quite obviously absurd and a pure invention. But what he must not do is be like Micah—testing the actual behavior of his listeners against the clear commandments of God, calling injustice by its true name on the basis of proved facts. But if he ever does refer to actual facts instead of merely spinning words, then let him please preach about wine and whiskey. That is the favorite subject of the army officers, officials, and soldiers. They will fit into their creed the stimulants for every taste, as gifts of the land, and hence the pledge and assurance of salvation. That is to say, to put it in plain terms, they will use this assurance for their own self-indulgent satisfaction.

This first pattern and example has showed us how the creed is misused, so that it turns into the mask which hides the true face of the addiction to pleasure. Here people are reckoning with God's patience where they themselves are concerned; but at the same time they are treating their neighbor as a greedy enemy would do. Here people are well aware of God's saving deeds; yet at the same time they are bringing terrible unhappiness to others unable to defend themselves. Here people are protesting at being called accursed; and at the same time they are treating their fellow men as if these were accursed. It is things like this that Micah reveals so ruthlessly.

The second scene is a brief one (3:1–4). The setting is Jerusalem. Here Micah is talking to those who are responsible for justice in Jerusalem. It is "their responsibility to foster justice" (3:1). But Micah is forced to accuse them because they "hate what is good and love what is evil." The duties of their office and their day-by-day exercise of those responsibilities are in sharp contrast to one another. Micah portrays this with a gross brutality which we find in none of the other prophets. Notice how in his metaphors he combines the butcher's bloody activity with the epicure's greed (3.2f.): "They eat the flesh of my people and break their bones in pieces, they tear the skin from off my people's flesh and the flesh from off their bones, they chop them up like meat for the cooking pot, like steaks for the frying pan." So he portrays the grimaces which accompany brutality and pleasure-seeking. People are treated like beasts for the slaughter. The people who are supposed to see that justice is done enjoy life at the expense of the ill-treated. This is the cannibalism of prosperity, and it has spread in Jerusalem to an unheard-of extent.

"And then—they cry unto Yahweh," Micah continues (3:4). Are they, too, putting on the mask of piety in order to hide the traces of blood and fat? Or are they themselves now in such need that they cannot find an escape route? In any case (3:4), "The Lord will not answer them. He will hide his face from them, because their deeds have been evil." They discover for themselves what Prov. 21:13 tells us: "He who closes his ear to the cry of the poor, will himself cry out and not be heard." So the

question faces every one of us: Does what we suffer perhaps correspond precisely to the suffering we have inflicted on other people—the suffering, that is to say, of not finding a hearing?

The third scene is a short one. Now prophets appear
(3:5). They are a different breed than the man from Moresheth.
3:11 indicates that they are officials, like the priests of the
Jerusalem Temple. So now, after the military leaders and the
judges, a religious class is exposed to the fire of criticism. Micah
immediately calls these prophets "seducers." Either they put
people on the wrong track, or they lead them into a state of intox-
ication in which they stagger on their feet and are no longer able
to walk straight toward a particular goal. Why have these people
become false guides? Micah does not deny that up to now they
have expected from God some answers to important questions
and have received guidance, too. But his reproach now is that
what they say is not in accordance with what they themselves
know to be God's directive. Micah says (3:5), "If they have
something to bite with their teeth, they cry *shalom* [peace,
prosperity, salvation]; but if a person refuses to give them what
they demand, they declare a holy war upon him." The word they
proclaim does not therefore depend on what they have ascertained
to be God's will; it depends on whether their listeners put a
special fee in their pockets. It is this discrepancy between the
word they have received and the word they proclaim which
makes them seducers. What comes out of their mouths depends
on what their listeners put into them. "Money talked louder then
God," as James L. Mays says. The prophet enjoyably enters into
his meal with relish, declaiming out of a full mouth the oracle
that assures his valued host of salvation; but anyone who meets
the prophet's private wishes with reserve receives bombastic
threats. The criterion for what the prophet says is his own selfish
interest, whatever would satisfy their own private whims. So we
hear later in the Lamentations after Jerusalem's downfall (Lam.
2:14): "Your prophets have seen for you false and deceptive visions; they have not exposed your iniquity so that you may repent, but have seen for you oracles false and misleading." Whoever occupies a preaching office or who strives after one cannot

be too clear about dangers of this kind. How easily the preacher holds his tongue about something essential, out of fear or out of false consideration for his listeners! How easily he stresses one point too much and holds back on another, out of self-interest! Only the sincere commitment to the word received by the first witnesses gives full freedom; it gives independence from contemporary threats and promises and points a plausible way to move into the future; in this way it is a real service of love to one's listeners.

What is Micah's threat against those who twist the word for their own purposes whenever they please (3:6f.): "It shall be night for you—without vision, darkness for you—without revelation. The sun is going down upon the prophets and dark shall the day be over them. Then the seers shall be disgraced, the diviners will have nothing to say; they shall all veil their mouths because they receive no response from God." That is to say, the people who from some time were able to really hear God's word will not be able to hear it any more. Anyone who falsifies the word, who distorts it, will have the word taken away from him. He will open the Scriptures, but they will no longer say anything to him. That is a harsh truth but an unequivocal one. It is a truth that the church of Christ and all who want to serve it have to allow this same word to speak now as it once spoke to the official prophets of Israel. The person who no longer takes his bearings from the word of the Lord will find it impossible to find his bearings at all. Dejected and shy, these people put their hands to their mouths and cover their moustaches, for they have nothing more to say. The men who have turned to inquiring and analyzing trends for themselves inquire about God's will in vain. "They receive no response from God." Here we discover why God can become a mute God. That always happens when his word is arbitrarily reinterpreted.

Now a highly important final scene follows (3:9–12). In this scene we find priests and judges together with the prophets. Here Micah confronts the mask and the true face more drastically than ever before. The word culminates in the severest threat against Jerusalem ever found in the whole Bible. So we ought to take this instance, drawn from a particular point in the history of God's people, as something not merely applying to Israel, but as even more applicable to the Christian church and all who are responsible for it. We should take it as a spur to self-examination in matters of hypocrisy and sincerity.

Micah immediately challenges the responsible authorities in Jerusalem concerning their faulty relationship to justice (3:9b): "You abhor justice and twist what is straight." Just like dirt and garbage are obnoxious to some, an orderly execution of justice was most obnoxious to the judges of Jerusalem. They find justice loathsome. Why? Because it stands in the way of their arbitrary behavior toward their fellow men. Certain Christian groups could find it needful to be reminded by the Old Testament that justice is a goodly order which should be observed; they should remember this when they brush it aside as "the law," appealing thereby to the gospel. When the voluntary principle is preached with high-sounding words but in fact a certain pressure is exerted, then that is nothing else than a refined version of that distorted justice which Micah denounces. "They twist what is straight." Isaiah talks about those who were experts at distortion (Isa. 5:20): "They put darkness for light and light for darkness, they put bitter for sweet, and sweet for bitter!" Constant vigilance is called for to see that a particular interpretation of the law does not end up poisoning that whole system of justice, above all at the cost of the defendant.

Micah produces evidence in the following for three flagrant perversions of the law.

1. They want to build up a proud, secure Zion and in doing so they mishandle people until they bleed (3:10): "They build Zion with blood and Jerusalem with unrighteousness." Toward the end of the eighth century B.C., under King Hezekiah, building activity reached immense proportions. Fortifications and public buildings as well as private houses sprang up like mushrooms (2 Chron. 32:27f.). The boring of the Siloam tunnel, which carries water from the Gichon spring under the city wall and into the inner city, was a technical achievement of the first rank. The tunnel was hewn out through the solid rocks for 1,700 feet, was about two feet wide and two to ten feet high. Micah brings out

the other side of the shield: these great technical achievements were bought with blood and evil actions. Here he is not only thinking of unavoidable, fatal construction accidents. He is thinking too of the nastiest, bloodiest ill-treatment by overseers and perhaps of the imposition of the death penalty. The picture of the butcher in 3:2-3, who cracks bones, goes back to actual horrendous experiences. Micah was perhaps drawing attention to the people from his own home, in their severe forced labor, when he says in 3:3, "They eat the flesh of my people." In 3:10 he says, "They build Zion with blood." Isaiah had said, "The Lord has founded Zion, and in her the afflicted of his people find refuge" (Isa. 14:32). But now justice and the life of the afflicted is being trampled down. It is being sacrificed to the pride of the elite, to military security, and to the progress of ever more luxurious living conditions. The alternative is clear: the pride and security for the great, or the right to life for the small. The problems involved were complicated then and are complicated today in their specifics; but the prophet takes sides without any ambiguity at all. Anyone who wants to follow in his footsteps will have to pay careful attention to the human needs which arise at every period when highly recommended projects earn enthusiastic praise.

2. Micah's decision is made even clearer by means of the second case of the violation of justice which he exposes: corruption and bribery. As far as the guilt of the people who are being attacked is concerned, it seems to have even more weight than the first, because this is ultimately the reason why the law has been twisted at all (3:11a): "Its leaders give judgment for a bribe; its priests interpret the law for pay; its prophets give their revelations for money." In this context, Micah has in mind the tormented people who have surrendered to a life without justice. They run from one place to the next making their appeal—from judge to priest, from priest to prophet—but they do not find support anywhere. For everywhere money is demanded. Money! Money! It stinks to high heaven. Micah uses three different words for money in this saying. In the case of the judges he calls it a bribe; it is secretly pushed into the folds of their clothing, into the judge's robe (Prov. 17:23). "The person who

gives a bribe always finds 'sympathy' for his position," says
Prov. 17:8. The word which Micah uses in the case of the priests
means the value, the price. So the priest's advice has become
venal too. We have already been told something similar about the
prophet: here he expects hard cash, pure and simple (silver).
The extent to which bribery reigns in all of the leading circles
in Jerusalem is appalling. The fascination of prosperity has
perverted all the rules of justice and all professional obligations.
The only morality is the morality of the good business deal. This
is the reason why the basic rights of the oppressed are in acute
danger. With his thrice-repeated pointer to financial greed,
Micah uncovers the real complexion of brutality and pleasure
seeking. He shows the leading motive of personal interest to be
more embarrassing than ever before. Just at this very point we
should avoid thinking or talking or listening as if this were something that only applied to other people. The right attitude
toward money cannot be critically enough examined by every individual. In our own time and at this point, efforts to control
ourselves as individual Christians and as a church should be still
more intensified. Micah shows how terribly close the twisting of
justice is to the receipt and spending of money.

3. But even worse than the true face of financial greed is the
mask which judges, priests, and prophets assume in all this—the
mask of an unshakable piety. This is the absolute limit, the pin-
nacle. They mean money, but they say "God." For Micah goes
on (3:11b): "But they lean upon Yahweh and say, 'Is not the
Lord in our midst? No evil shall come upon us!'" That is how
they reject Micah's threat of disaster, too. They think they are
immune. To lean upon Yahweh—that is the expression of an unshakable trust in God. "Is not the Lord in our midst?" In saying
this they are referring back to psalms like the forty-sixth: "The
Lord of hosts is with us; the God of Jacob is our refuge." Are
they perhaps subjectively sincere? Are they making their faith a
private matter, forgetting that God is the God of other people
too? They do not notice the contradiction between their repudia-
tion of justice, their dedication to financial gain, and their verbal
devotion to Yahweh. This should make all later listeners to
Micah reckon all the more clearly with the possibility that state-

ments of faith may become the slogans of religious self-security; and for Micah this is the very peak of the indictment. Hypocrisy in religious profession is added to injustice against men and women and to the greed for money; and this hypocrisy is really a denial of the God of Israel as the God of all the wretched. He is pushed out as the Lord both of one's own life and also as the one who stands by all who suffer. That is why trust in God of this kind is a dreadful mask. Micah testifies that God himself rips off this mask.

For this is how his saying ends (3:12): "Therefore [therefore!] because of you Zion will be plowed as a field, Jerusalem shall become a heap of ruins, and the temple mount will be given over to the beasts of the forest." This judgment must have burst like a bomb when Micah hurled it against the judges, the priests, and the prophets: Because of you! A pile of rubble! A heap of ruins! A wilderness, left to the howls of jackals and hyenas! That is what will happen to the proud city, the city they wanted to build with blood. Never in history has Jerusalem been threatened with anything worse than this.

Do you notice how Micah never mentions Yahweh at this point? Yahweh's name is intoned over and over from behind the masks of Micah's opponents: "Is not Yahweh in our midst?" "They put their trust in Yahweh" (3:11). "They cry to Yahweh" (3:4). "Is Yahweh impatient?" (2:7). Micah, on the other hand, uses a restrained passive form. "Zion will be plowed as a field" (3:12). He only talks about the "mountain of the house" (3:12), not about "the house of Yahweh." Nor does he begin in 3:12 with "Thus says Yahweh." This "messenger formula" is added later, in Jer. 26:18. The piously smug, unctuous speech of the others has probably forced Micah to exert unusual reserve in the use of God's name. He hardly ever mentions the name of God, "Yahweh." We should take this to heart and compare it with Jesus' rejection of the people who only say "Lord, Lord!" but do not do the will of his Father.

So where is God's presence now to be found, if it is no longer in his own city, no longer in his temple—if it is no longer to be discovered where he once allowed himself to be approached? The Lord has bound his presence not to the place but to the word. In the word of justice and in its witness, Micah, he remains present in the midst of God's dark ways and all the divine dumbness in the mouths of the false prophets. He remains efficaciously present in his very judgment as the one who acts silently, but is still testified to by some individuals whom he has touched.

A hundred years later, at Jeremiah's trial, the elders of Judah remember that King Hezekiah listened to the voice of that one individual by the name of Micah. Hezekiah changed his ways not only in his speech, but in his total life; he let himself be guided by the God of Micah, the prophet. Micah's word has been effective among us now for twenty-seven centuries. What lasting change can it effect for us in our time? May Micah help us take off the masks of pious speech and turn instead to the blessing of a straightforward and unambiguous life. Let him do his unmasking work!

4

WHAT IS NEW IN THE NEW COVENANT?

A Contribution to the Jewish-Christian Dialogue According to Jer. 31:31–34

WHEN THE AMERICAN Holocaust film was shown on German television screens, millions of people watching in their own living rooms felt a sense of shock and horror. There were long discussions. But the most important question still has to be settled. Auschwitz and the mass murder of countless Jews has to become a burning question not only for Germans as such, but especially for all Christians. How do we all share in that guilt? How can we stop a new hate against the Jews? When we are trying to break down tensions in the world of nations, what can a new brotherhood between Jews and Christians teach us?

Let us go to the root of the matter at once. The main source of the antagonism between Jews and Christians lies in their different interpretations of the Bible. Do we want anything more than tolerant coexistence? Do we want to arrive at a brotherly cooperation which can become a model for peace between nations? If we do, we shall have to seek a discussion with Israel about the Bible which has the goal of mutual understanding. For this present occasion I suggest listening to the prophecy concerning the new covenant which the Book of Jeremiah tells us about in Chapter 31, verses 31 to 34. Christians have often appropriated these verses only for themselves far too hastily and quite wrongly. On the other hand, as far as I can see, the Jews have paid too little attention to these verses even though their primary concern is only applied to Israel herself.

Let us look at verse 31: "Behold, the days are coming, says the Lord, when I will make a new covenant with the house of Israel

49

and the house of Judah." This first sentence brings us face to face with two questions. We shall take these questions with us on our journey of discovery through the whole passage. "Behold, the days are coming . . ." When are they coming? Have they already come? Are we still waiting for them? That is the first question—a question of burning tension between Jews and Christians. The second question is this: what is essentially new about the new covenant? We shall be looking out for a clear answer to this question in what follows. It will be well if we can find one. For we can only find an answer to our first question if we can answer the second one. We hope we shall be able to answer it. We shall have to compare that which is proclaimed as new, feature by feature, with the realities of our situation today.

In addition to these two questions, the first sentence also gives us two basic indicators to guide our way. "Behold, the days are coming, *says the Lord.*" The phrase "says the Lord" is reiterated in each of the following verses—at the end of verse 32 and then again in the middle of both verses 33 and 34. This shows that we are supposed to hear the whole statement as a promise of God. This is stressed four times. It is in line with this, too, that in most sentences God's own "I" is the subject: "I will make a new covenant"; "I will put my law within them"; "I will forgive their iniquity"; and so on. That is to say, from the very beginning the new covenant can only be understood as the free gift of God's promise. This is true whether we reckon with God in other ways or whether we do not reckon with him at all. This new covenant can only be understood if we discover it as God's will and his act. It remains incomprehensible if we only deal with it as a kind of human fellowship or community, even a fellowship of a religious kind. "Thus says the Lord"—that is the indispensable presupposition for the understanding of the new covenant.

The other basic indicator concerns the people to whom the promise is addressed. In verse 31 we read: "I will make a new covenant with the house of *Israel* and the house of *Judah.*" Compare that with verse 33! There it is only "the house of Israel" that is mentioned. How is this difference to be explained? It seems to me most probable that, according to verse 33, at first only Israel was addressed, whereas in verse 31 "and the house of

Judah" was added at a later point. This textual observation is an interesting one. In the period before the exile, Israel and Judah were the names of two separate states. Israel was the name of the northern kingdom, and Samaria was its capital. The southern kingdom was called Judah, and its capital was Jerusalem. In 722 B.C. Israel, the northern kingdom, was completely destroyed, and most of the survivors were deported. It was precisely this miserable remnant to whom the new covenant was promised first of all. Then, in 587 B.C., the state of Judah was destroyed, too. The sanctuary in Jerusalem was burned down, and large numbers of Judah's people were forcibly deported. It was after this that the promise given to Israel was applied also to the house of Judah by a new prophetic voice. You see, text and literary criticism do not have the goal of excluding some words from the text, but to learn how the living word works further on in new generations and in other people. In other words, the prophetic saying touched the different sections of the ancient people of God one after another in the wake of their utter collapse. These were times of complete despair and total resignation. The pathetic remnant was at the point of burying its final hopes in exile. Then its sights were raised high once more: "Behold, the days are coming, . . . when I will make a new covenant."

Let us remember first of all that the saying about the new covenant initially was promised to Israel and later to Judah. That is to say, at first it did not apply to just any random groups belonging to the other nations. Even less can there be any question of the new covenant applying first of all to Christians. Christians have sometimes called themselves "the people of the new covenant," arrogantly setting themselves above the people of the old covenant. This is conceit of the most impudent kind, and it has had terrible consequences. We must impress one thing on ourselves: not only is Israel the people of the old covenant, the new covenant too was promised in the first place to Israel and Israel alone. The power of this promise has preserved Israel as a people of a special kind in spite of all the catastrophes that have happened to her. The very fact that there are still Jews today, in spite of everything, actually points to the fact that God is true to his promise.

When Jesus' ministry began he, Jesus the Jew, knew that he

was sent only to "the lost sheep of the house of Israel" (Matt. 15:24). It was only as the risen Christ, then, that he gave the charge to his disciples—all of whom were Jews!—"Go and make disciples of all nations!" (Matt. 28:19). Paul the Jew then showed the congregations who were drawn from the non-Jewish nations how to find help for themselves in the Old Testament, which was written for Israel. In this way the Gentile congregation too would be permitted to come alive to the promise of the new covenant. It would recall the first two groups to whom the promise was originally addressed, and it would give renewed thought to the fact that the word was applied in the despairing atmosphere of eclipse and extinction that hung over God's people in their disintegration. No feelings of superiority allegedly based on the New Testament can raise their head here. On the contrary, the promise will bring the Christian community into the profoundest solidarity with Israel and its distress, especially in periods of affliction, uncertainty, and hopelessness. It will put an end to the arrogance which kindled the massive burnt offerings which weigh so inexpressibly on us as Germans. It will give way to a thankful humility. Paul teaches us this in the words to the Romans: "It is not you that support the root, but the root that supports you" (Rom. 11:18). So it is only very much as latecomers that we are listening in on the word which was addressed originally to Israel and Judah. Still, together with the Jewish people we may and should now hear what the new covenant is about.

First of all, in verse 32, the prophet explains what the new covenant is *not:* "Not like the covenant which I made with their fathers when I took them by the hand to bring them out of the land of Egypt." Up to this point nothing negative has been said about the old covenant. On the contrary, it is emphasized that the old covenant too was the result of God's gracious initiative, and that its chief distinguishing sign—its trademark—was the liberation from Egypt. The old covenant also was a covenant of grace and deliverance. But what then made the old covenant really old? What made it no longer valid? What makes a new one necessary? The sequel in verse 32 tells us: "my covenant, which they broke, though I was their husband, says the Lord." That is the point. Israel has broken the covenant which brought with it the promises of Yahweh. Israel has destroyed the covenant— dissolved it, annulled it—even though the Lord has remained faithful to it. We find a precise interpretation of our sentence "they broke my covenant" in Jer. 11:10: "They have turned back to the iniquities of their forefathers, who refused to hear my words; they have gone after other gods to serve them; [in this way] the house of Israel and the house of Judah have broken my covenant which I made with their fathers." So the prophet makes the point absolutely clearly and unequivocally: it is not God the Lord who has put an end to the old covenant, it is Israel. But that means the covenant no longer exists. In saying this the prophet is only saying what every one of the great prophets had testified to and had told Israel from the eighth century on. Hosea actually proclaimed in his God's name (Hos. 1:9), "You are not my people and I am not your God"; Amos 8:2 testified, "The end has come upon my people Israel"; and Isa. 1:2f. states, "Sons have I reared and brought up, but they have rebelled against me. The ox knows his owner, and the ass his master's crib, but Israel does not know, my people do not understand." So the great prophecy we find in the Old Testament is far, far more than an interpretation of the Torah. It reveals to Israel how it has dissolved the old cove- nant. They have separated themselves from the hand of the one who wanted to lead them to liberty and life. Amos showed how they have made the grasping of injustice their guiding principle instead of God's good precepts. Hosea lays bare how they pledged themselves to the life of sultry Canaanite sexual rites instead of fellowship with their God. Isaiah denounced the way they longed for freedom through military treaties with the major powers instead of through trust in the Lord of all powers. So they have broken the old covenant by forsaking their God.

And yet Israel's God still shows himself to be the Lord. He holds fast to his people even in wrath. He leads the nations to chastise his people. In heartrending words, the prophets wit- ness to the divine wrath. But God's wrath descends equally on the nations when they fall upon his unfaithful people indepen- dently and of their own accord. So Isaiah says (10:15), "Shall the axe vaunt itself over him who hews with it, or the saw magnify against him who wields it?'' So Christians belonging to the Gentile nations would do well to see themselves together with Israel in the mirror of prophecy, in a mirror reflecting the history of the old covenant's disintegration. Here both Jews and Christians learn what it means to let go of the hand which leads us to freedom. Here nothing must be forgotten, and nothing is to be hushed up.

Our prophet proclaimed without any ambiguity whatsoever that the old covenant had been broken. So the declaration of the new covenant, already announced in Jer. 31:31, is all the more surprising. What is new about this new covenant? We read in 31:33, "But this is the covenant which I will make with the house of Israel after those days, says the Lord: I will put my law within them, and I will write it upon their hearts; and I will be their God, and they shall be my people." Again, let us see first of all in what ways the new covenant is like the old one. There are three points to notice. First, "I will!" It is God's gracious initiative which brings forth the new covenant just as it once did the old one. Second, the basis of the new covenant is "the law," that is to say the Torah, as the guide to help us on our way—the same basis as of the old one. Third, the goal of the new covenant is the same as the goal of the old one: "I will be their God, and they shall be my people" (31:33b).

But what is new—new and unprecedented—is the way in which God's guiding directions are to be mediated. "I will put my law *within them*, and I will write it *upon their hearts*." That is the first completely new element in this new covenant. How different from the old way of the transmission of the commandments, when the tablets on Sinai were set up before Israel, written and fixed! What a tremendous distance! We are told in Exod. 20:18ff. that in its deadly fear Israel could not endure the voice of God and begged Moses to become their go-between. How different it was even when the priest proclaimed the will of God! How different, even, when a man wrote the commandment on the doorposts of his house and on his gates or when he actually bound them as a sign on his forehead and on his hand (Deuteronomy 6). In all such cases, the expectation of the commandments was set up over against the achievement of obedience. Even when (accord-

ing to Deut. 6:6) a person himself takes to heart God's com-
mands—even then there is still an open, severe conflict. For according to Jer. 17:1, there was another writing already chiseled in the
heart: "The sin of Judah is written with a pen of iron; with a
point of diamond it is engraved on the tablet of their heart."
Jeremiah above all was acutely aware of how a person is impris-
oned within his own inner contradictions. "Can the Ethiopian
change his skin or the leopard his spots? Then also you can do
good who are accustomed to do evil," he says in 13:23. Jeremiah
sees the problem of the old covenant as being an entirely anthropological one: when it really comes to the point, man is incapable
of obedience.

It is precisely here that the newness of the new covenant takes
shape. The instruction no longer comes from the outside to confront man. God's command now fulfills and molds man's inner-
most longings, his will. The gap between God's addressing man
on the one hand and man's obedience on the other is bridged,
and the heart is directly fashioned by God's call to freedom.
God's own finger inscribes the heart—the organ which gives life
its direction.

Ezekiel described even more precisely and clearly the new,
revolutionary quality of what Jeremiah means. What he proclaims
is a heart transplant: the heart of stone which is impervious to
impressions will be surgically removed, and a new heart of flesh,
living and functioning, will be implanted instead. God's Spirit
itself is the pulsating life of this new heart (Ezek. 11:19 and
36:26). Then the conflict between willing and doing is eradicated
in a positively anatomical way. God's goodwill is completely
united with the human will. Then we are no longer "righteous
and sinners at the same time" (*simul justus et peccator*); then we
are not just different in part (inwardly or outwardly, or centrally
or peripherally); we are totally different from what we were
before. Then, as Kornelis H. Miskotte puts it, "the newest of the
new is present: the new man, a heart such as there has never been
before on this earth."

So that is the first newness in the new covenant. Concerning
that, we now ask: does this new covenant proclaimed in Jeremiah
apply to the present in what it says about the entirely new heart?

Is this new heart a present reality? As a Christian community, are we completely united with the will of God in that sense? We have to confess with Israel that we are still waiting for fulfillment. Like Israel we have to underline what verse 33a says, which applies to us as well—"after those days." At the moment we are still both righteous and sinners.

But that is not everything that has to be said. We have to ask our friends from Israel: what do you have to say to your Jewish brothers who make themselves heard in the New Testament, telling that one has arisen in their midst whom they have seen and heard, whom their hands have touched, and in whom they have recognized the newest of the new in bodily form—the new man, Jesus of Nazareth? From him they heard the convincing statement: "My food is to do the will of him who sent me, and to accomplish his work" (John 4:34). And in Gethsemane he cried: "Father, not my will but thine be done" (Luke 22:42). It is not in our hearts but in his heart that we recognize the handwriting of God himself. It is in him that we Christians see the reality of the new covenant in our midst. There is more. Through him we see the new covenant realized for us, on our behalf. For that is what the New Testament witnesses from Israel—our apostles—have transmitted on to us from his Last Supper: that he gave his blood to be the blood of the new covenant for the many. There Exodus 24 and Jeremiah 31 are contracted: "The new covenant in my blood" (Luke 22:20). So in spite of our still divided hearts we believe that he has actually put into force for us what verse 33b tells us is the goal of the covenant: "I will be their God, and they shall be my people." We are permitted to be sure that we have been called to be God's people in the name of Jesus—called with Jesus' Jewish messengers and with the brethren from Israel who are alive today. Apart from Jesus' name we certainly do not have this assurance; in that name we just as certainly do have it. In Rom. 9:25 we can read that the people whom Hosea was bound to call "not my people" are now again—or for the first time—called "my people."

Something else follows from this as well. Under the influence of Jesus' word there are, here and there, actually traces of God's handwriting in our hearts already. In the church there is a provisional blazing up of the end time. In the midst of our inner conflict we may daily pray and expect that his Spirit will overcome our stubborness. This gives us a foretaste of being finally united with his love and liberty. Paul calls it a "guarantee" (2 Cor. 1:22; 5:5)—like a pledge or a downpayment, a first installment—which Jesus' Spirit is beginning to bring about among us and which assures us of the complete installation of a new heart which is yet to come. So we live between the covenants, as it were. Or better, we live on the steps which lead to the fulfillment of the new covenant.

Let us sum up provisionally. We have seen that the first element that is totally new in the new covenant is the heart on which God himself has written; that is to say, the complete renewal of our conscience, our will, and our passions through God himself. In Jesus we see this newest-of-the-new realized and present in our midst. With him, therefore, the time which Jeremiah 31 announces as the coming time has actually arrived. In him, the new covenant is present. With him, the end of time has begun. For ourselves, for the church of Jews and Gentiles, we perceive it fragmentarily, as an advance payment. Along with Israel we are waiting for its completion. And yet through Jesus we are all now, in the present, already actually called to be God's new people—called again or called for the first time.

The transitional state between the beginning and the consummation of the end time becomes even clearer in the final verse of our text. First of all, we hear what the second new aspect about the new covenant is (31:34a): "No longer shall each man teach his neighbor and each his brother, saying, 'Know the Lord,' for they shall all know me, from the least of them to the greatest, says the Lord." What does this mean? Do not be alarmed! Rather, rejoice all the more about this aspect. For it means nothing less than the final end of the teaching profession. That is the obvious result of God's own inscribing of man's heart. The prophet is probably thinking about the utter futility of teaching in the days of King Josiah and the Deuteronomic reform. Some of us could perhaps also find something to say about the futility of teaching. At that time the eagerness to teach must have been astonishing.

And yet it could not produce the new person, just as little as later efforts to instruct could do so. But now we are told that in the new covenant, "they shall know me from the least to the greatest" —everyone—children and scholars, the educated and the simple, the independent and the dependent. All these differences will become inessential. Only one thing will matter: "Know the Lord!" In the Bible "knowing" means something quite different from a fleeting acquaintanceship, or even from the painstaking but detached noting of a fact where detachment is actually proclaimed as being the necessary condition for knowing at all. In the Bible it is quite different. There knowing means gathering the experiences of love, becoming more and more intimate from day to day, and having living fellowship with our friend. We know in the same measure as we love. So when God promises "They shall all know me," this means "they will live on the strength of an intimate contact with me, they will acquire immediate and reliable insight into my ways, and they will experience complete, living fellowship with me." The new covenant was initiated solely on God's side, but now it really becomes a two-way covenant: every individual is in complete harmony with him, the One. There will be no need for teachers as go-betweens, but rather there will be complete harmony with the whole people of God.

It is equally clear to Jews and Christians alike that this second aspect of the newness belongs to the consummation for which we are still waiting. But when we are inspired by this expectation of the future, our mutual instruction and exhortation will simply cease to be relevant; and then this expectation—expectation in the form of hope—can do two things.

First of all, it will continually bring us face to face with the provisional nature of what we now teach and know; we can no doubt sigh over our blunders as teachers or students, but we need not give up completely on this learning process and on our teaching activities. For through it all we are stumbling towards the full knowledge of God. He has promised us, "They shall all know me." That is our comfort.

And the second point: this expectation does not permit any fanatic legalism or any vain conceit. On the journey to the new covenant of perfected fellowship, the basic attitude in the provisional teaching profession cannot be to control the faith, but only that we may help others find joy: "We work with you for your joy" (2 Cor. 1:24). In this way this transitional period of ours ought to be released from its tensions—in the mutual instruction of Christians and Jews, too. For it is a period of anticipatory joy: "They shall all know me." They will all be my familiar, trusted friends.

But now we come to the third point, after the lifesaving heart surgery and after the dissolution of the teaching profession. We find the third aspect of the newness of the new covenant in verse 34b: "I will forgive their iniquity, and I will remember their sin no more." Are we capable of thinking through what a complete change of direction this promise of the forgiveness of sins makes in the history of our lives? This radical alteration is as great as the final judgment of the world. The forgiveness of sins promised here is the here-and-now anticipation of the Last Judgment. It means a valid verdict of not guilty at the Last Judgment. The words for iniquity and sin in Hebrew really mean "confusion" and "aberration." But "to forgive" means to pardon completely; it is a complete cancellation of all our contempt of God and his will, and the restoration of friendship. "No more remember" is a legal term which really means no longer bringing the evil thing before any court of law; it means dropping the case once and for all. In short, the final sentence is a firm promise that in the new covenant God will cast all occasions of wrath and punishment "into the deepest depths of the sea," in the splendid words of Mic. 7:19—the place where Israel's bitterest enemies, the chariots of Egypt, sank out of sight forevermore. That is what the forgiveness of sins really means: to be saved from our most dangerous enemies in the face of judgment, to be given a free pardon for our worst offenses.

Here we are at the very apex of the new covenant—no, we really have to say this is the foundation of the new covenant. It is a basis the old covenant knew nothing about. Here it is well worth our while to observe this most carefully. In what way is the promise of the forgiveness of sins the bedrock of the new covenant? Verse 34b is a causal clause; it begins with *ki*, which means "for" or "because." What statement is the clause justifying with this "for"?

1. First of all, undoubtedly the clause justifies the sentence that immediately precedes it (34a): the knowledge of God grows out of the forgiveness of sins. Without the forgiveness of sins there is no knowledge of God. But the forgiveness of sins is the reason for the essential knowledge of God because it is the experience of love. To recognize God as the one who takes away the devastating power of confusion and aberration truly means to discover him. This, therefore, is the first statement which is being established here: the forgiveness of sins is the reason behind the knowledge of God.

2. But the causal clause undoubtedly goes further back as well: it makes the new covenant even possible for the very first time. We have to remember the sin expressly named in verse 32b. The old covenant has been broken; Israel has abandoned and betrayed its liberator and has turned to idols. The forgiveness of this main sin, the dropping of this crucial case, this chief indictment, makes the new promise even a possibility for the very first time. So the forgiveness of sins creates the absolute presupposition for the new covenant. It is quite simply the new covenant's cornerstone.

3. Finally, we should notice that the reason given here functions as the closing sentence. This means that we are certainly intended to relate it to the future. It is the justification for the permanence of the new covenant. The promise of the forgiveness of sins does not only anticipate all human achievement and merit, it also anticipates all the foreseeable failure of the old and the new people of God. The assurance of the forgiveness of sins guarantees the steadfastness, the indestructibility of the new covenant. Thus the old broken-down covenant is not renewed. What is being established is a covenant that is genuinely new in kind, a covenant that is steadfast and which no sin can ever demolish. That is why when Jer. 32:40 picks up our promise, the passage goes on—and this is very interesting and very important—to talk about an everlasting covenant: "I will make with

them an everlasting covenant, that I will not turn away from doing good to them."

We now have to ask about the "when" of the time that is to come. Up to now we have seen that the whole new man of the new heart has appeared in our history in Jesus. For us he is present hope. The end of the teaching profession is a pure dream of the future if we do not want to turn into mere enthusiasts. But the promise of the forgiveness of sins has already been historically realized in Jesus, and it is already a complete reality in the present. It draws a definite, final line under all of our past life. So for the time being and until the day of fulfillment, we remain both righteous and sinners simultaneously. The forgiveness promised to us is the reason for each one of us being filled every morning with astonishment over the world and over oneself, and over being allowed to begin anew *in* the new covenant *in the direction* of the new covenant, in the tension between the fulfillment in Jesus and the consummation for ourselves, for the community drawn from Israel, and for the nations.

There is one question we still have to ask our Jewish brethren. The New Testament tells us about the Jews who found the new covenant of the forgiveness of sins historically documented in Jesus' Passover supper and his crucifixion. If we consider this in the light of the history of the tradition, were the ideas and perceptions of these people not precisely in line with the Old Testament accounts of the making of the covenant and the prophetic promises? Can one as a Jew really read the New Testament message about the justification of the godless as being anything other than the sealing of the prophetic promise of the new covenant?

Perhaps a final little impetus is necessary. The proper mobility is lacking for the conversation between Jews and Christians if we stop short at the Torah and the Talmud on the one hand, and at Jesus and the New Testament on the other. We can put our foot on a bridge of encounter when we think about prophecy together, the prophecy which is given at first to Israel, and when we consider the eschatological revolution in biblical prophecy, especially the message about the radically new thing which we find in prophecy at the beginning and the end of the exilic period.

Here as Christians we discover the roots of our faith which bind us to Israel in an indissoluble bond. Could not the Jewish people, too, come closer to us today if they were able to see Jeremiah's new covenant not merely as the renewal of the old one, but as the promised covenant of hope—a covenant of a radically new kind? Is not prophecy pointing quite unambiguously beyond the Torah when Isa. 43:18f. cries to us: "Remember not the former things, nor consider the things of old! Behold, I am doing a new thing"?

But these are doctrinal questions. What is more important is the fact that the proclamation of the new covenant for Jews and Christians is in effect now, in the mode of promise and in the mode of fulfillment. How, after Auschwitz, could we allow ourselves even to come face to face with a single Jew if it were not for the forgiveness of trespasses?

The necessity of forgiveness and its power urge us on to think about new conditions in the divided world of the nations and to experiment. The experience of forgiveness is not merely a private affair. In the biblical sense it is a matter for the world. The experience of forgiveness as the bedrock of the new covenant excludes vengeance on every level. This means that Christians will have to learn to practice a policy of going forward to meet the other, a policy of concession and cooperation. With every first step toward renouncing retaliation, the newest-of-the-new enters history. Apart from a policy which thinks consistently in the light and in the direction of the new covenant, there will hardly be any hope at all for this old world. Exactly as Christians, we have to think about this—and to vote.

5

HOW CAN WE RECOGNIZE FALSE PROPHETS?

Criteria for the Difficult Task of Testing the Spirits

WE ARE FACED nowadays with violently contradictory views on questions which are of vital importance to us all. Our common future is at stake. And yet confusion and conflict are spreading at the very points where, now more than ever, agreement and cooperation are essential. But what is true, and what is false?

In the Old Testament the explosive force of questions like these erupts when touched by the kindling touch of prophecy. Let us first of all be clear about what we mean by prophecy. Prophecy moves present behavior into the light of future events, and it does so in the name of God. Isa. 30:15–17 will make clear what I mean by this: "Thus says the Lord, the Holy One of Israel: 'Only by returning and by resting shall you be saved; only quietness and trust shall give you strength!' But you would not; you said: 'No! we will speed upon horses!'—therefore you shall speed away!—and: 'We will ride upon swift steeds!'—therefore your pursuers shall be swifter!" What does this mean? We have here a statement of two opposing positions. *Israel* expects that an alliance with Egypt and its corps of chariots, which were the swiftest and strongest in the ancient orient, will save the country from Assyria, the hostile power from the East. But *Isaiah* warns his people that the Assyrians are stronger still. *Israel*, probably encouraged by other prophets and priests, imagines that it can resist Assyria with the help of a military pact with Egypt. *Isaiah*, on the other hand, pleads with his people to lie low, consistently and resolutely, and to turn to their God—the political consequence being strict neutrality. This, then, is what prophecy is: it is not some kind of fortune-telling; it is judgment about the pres-

ent in the light of the future—judgment arrived at in obedience to
the will of God.

It is not only the *Old* Testament which is familiar with prophecy in this sense. Luke 13:34f. tells us that *Jesus* cried to Jerusalem: "O Jerusalem, Jerusalem, killing the prophets and stoning
those who are sent to you! How often would I have gathered your
children together, as a hen gathers her chickens under her wings;
but you would not! Behold your house is forsaken." And Luke
19:43f. goes on: "Your enemies will hem you in on every side.
They will dash you and your children to pieces and will not leave
one stone upon another." This is what prophecy is: judgment
about the present in the light of the future—judgment arrived at
through the authority of God. But it is not only Jesus who comes
forward as prophet in New Testament times.

Prophecy played a very important part also in the early years of
the Christian community. According to Matt. 23:24, Jesus did
not merely send out teachers or wise men as his disciples; he sent
prophets as well. They were probably itinerant prophets, for
Matt. 10:41 says: "He who receives a prophet because he is a
prophet shall receive a prophet's reward." But Jesus is aware of
deceptive, fraudulent prophets too. His admonition in the Sermon on the Mount (Matt. 7:15): "Beware of false prophets!"
makes this evident. Prophets have always been disputed people.
Still, in spite of the fact that prophecy can be faked, the early
Christians, as disciples of Jesus, considered prophecy to be completely indispensible as judgment concerning the present world
situation in the light of Jesus' message about the coming kingdom of God. Paul admonishes his readers (1 Thess. 5:20f.):
"Do not despise prophetic speaking! Test everything and hold
fast to the good!" Warnings of this kind show how necessary it
is—in fact indispensible—to distinguish between true and false
prophecy. Everyone has to learn that *false prophets have to be
reckoned with* and that they must be distinguished from the true
ones. This is an educational process, a matter of training, and it
is not the New Testament alone that requires us to undergo it.
The prophetic books of the Old Testament offer us instructive
examples. Let us look at them attentively. For the prophetic office is both a dangerous office and an endangered one. The ex-

amples I have given already suggest that it is closely bound up with the question of true or false political preaching. Jesus says in the Sermon on the Mount (Matt. 7:15): "The false prophets come to you like [harmless] sheep; but in reality they are ravening wolves." Nowadays we hear on the one hand that everything that takes place on the military and political level is merely intended to serve the cause of peace; on the other hand we discover that the military measures that have already been taken are sufficient to destroy the whole of mankind several times over. It is urgently necessary for us to develop keen consciences which have learned to see through false prophets.

It is sobering to discover from the Old Testament that "testing the spirits" is not merely *necessary*; it is also extremely *difficult*. So we should not be surprised if it seems to us perplexingly complicated to arrive at a proper judgment about the future and to make the right decision about the present. Yet it is vitally necessary for people of all age groups to do so, especially younger people. No single one of us can evade the difficulty of the task simply by looking to see what the speaker's official position is, as if the people entrusted with some office in the church were always true witnesses and independent lay helpers, for example, were false ones from the very outset—or vice versa. Amos was undoubtedly a true prophet; yet he declares explicitly that originally he was not a prophet at all and that he did not belong to any prophetic guild. He earned his living by breeding cattle and growing figs. But, he tells us, the Lord, the God of Israel, had called him irresistibly to expose Israel's guilt and announce her downfall (Amos 7:14f.). On the other hand we find Micah surrounded by prophets who were officially appointed as such in Jerusalem, like the priests and judges (Mic. 3:11). But Micah says that these prophets make themselves inexcusably dependent upon other people, and that they will therefore end up in darkness and uncertainty of mind, unable to receive and pass on a divine answer to the burning questions of the day. True or false— the answer to this has never depended on a recognition of official social position. This makes the decision genuinely difficult and forces us all to arrive at an independent judgment. A church that claims to believe in the priesthood of all believers must reckon with truly prophetic voices from all sections of society. A pastor or bishop is not equipped with prophetic authority simply by virtue of his office, and politicians or statesmen are not to be rejected just because they are not ordained theologians. The word of each and all of them has to be tested in its own right.

But distinguishing true prophecy from false involves a greater difficulty even than this. We must not try to save ourselves from an initial uncertainty. The Old Testament tells us in one passage that the God of Israel lets prophets be overtaken by a "spirit of lies." In 1 Kings 22, the kings of Israel and Judah ask a whole parliament of four hundred prophets whether they can and should wage a campaign against the Aramaeans, and whether such a campaign would be successful. The four hundred give an encouraging reply, and one of them, Zedekiah, confirms this answer by the symbolic act of putting on an ox's horns made of iron and saying: "In this way you will strike Aram down and destroy it." But in spite of the confirmatory sign and the massive assent, the advice proves to be false. And, conversely, it is only a single individual, Micaiah ben Imlah, who exposes the deception after the king of Israel has repeatedly put the question to him. Micaiah declares that the king himself is going to fall in battle, and that his people will return home in confusion. God has first of all permitted a lying spirit to fall upon the other prophets. Zedekiah protests, and Micaiah is thrown into prison. But his prophecy comes true for all that. Let us notice here that a single individual proves to be right and four hundred prove to be wrong. The person who seems to be so superior and who behaves with such bombastic self-confidence turns out to be a liar. The king only learns the truth after repeated inquiry—only when it is quite clear that he does not simply want to have his own wishes confirmed, but is genuinely trying to find out what the will of God really is. Then the truth comes to light. Distinguishing between true and false prophecy can therefore be a difficult and prolonged process; we may waver in our opinion, we may feel uncertain. Persevering, exhaustive questioning is required of us, not a hasty and strident judgment. People who come forward with special self-assurance must be scrutinized particularly critically and compared with their opponents. "Testing the spirits" is certainly anything but child's play.

False prophecy can therefore be a trial sent by God to test us; it can mean agonizing assailment. Even a man like the prophet Jeremiah sometimes felt cheated by his God. Under the weight of God's hand he saw himself as totally isolated. The opponents he had threatened were laughing at him triumphantly. For a long time it was they and not Jeremiah who seemed to have been proved right, as the calamity Jeremiah proclaimed failed to materialize. In this extremity Jeremiah cries to God (Jer. 15:18): "You have become to me like a deceitful brook, like waters which do not keep their word" (the bed of a stream promises refreshing water, but when we come closer to it, it has nothing to offer). It is the true prophets most of all who have to pass through tormenting periods of waiting, endless loneliness, and bitter temptation. These are already a distant foreshadowing of Jesus' suffering from Gethsemane to the cross.

If we look at these difficulties properly—these trials endured by the biblical messengers—it can become apparent to us on closer examination that the task of distinguishing is not only essential and not merely painful, but that it is also a *possible* task, one capable of being successfully completed. The biblical testimonies make it plain that the last word must not be left to the depression and resignation which laments that, when all is said and done, no one really knows what the right course is. The story of Jeremiah's life allows us to trace the steps that led him from profound uncertainty to new assurance. Chapters 27 and 28 offer an illuminating example.

The incident they describe took place during King Zedekiah's reign, around 593 B.C. Nebuchadnezzar II had captured Jerusalem for the first time in 597. The reigning king of the time, Jehoiachin, had been carried off into exile in Babylon, and the precious temple vessels had been seized as spoils of war. Zedekiah had been installed as royal vassal by Nebuchadnezzar's favor. After about four years, a kind of foreign ministers' conference was held in Jerusalem. Representatives of the neighboring states of Edom, Moab, Ammon, Tyre, and Sidon gathered together in Judah's capital in order to discuss a possible rebellion against the Babylonian Empire. Then Jeremiah appears on the scene demonstratively, carrying an ox's yoke on his neck and saying, in effect, in his God's name: "I, Yahweh, have given your countries into the hand of my servant [sic!] Nebuchadnezzar. All your peoples must submit to him. They are to put their necks under his yoke. The prophets who say anything different are liars. The subjection is to last for at least two to three generations until the time of Nebuchadnezzar's son and grandson." So much for Jeremiah's proclamation. After a while another prophet appears, a man called Hananiah. Echoing Jeremiah's own style and picking up his symbol of the ox's yoke, Hananiah solemnly proclaims, as the messenger of his God: "Thus says the Lord Sabaoth, the God of Israel: I will break the yoke of the king of Babylon. The precious vessels belonging to the temple will be brought back after only two years and King Jehoiachin will return home, together with all the people who have been deported." Hananiah makes this prediction in the presence of all the people and the priests assembled in front of the temple. There can be no doubt that he was applauded by court circles and by the vast majority of the anti-Babylonian party in Jerusalem and its allied states.

So what was Jeremiah's position now? The conflict with his own professional colleagues must have been one of the hardest struggles ever inflicted on him. We sense that at first Hananiah's intervention took his breath away. At all events he is not immediately able to call on a divine word with which to refute the self-confident Hananiah. Nor does he revert to his own saying, with the accompanying yoke symbol, which he had proclaimed in the name of his God. On the contrary, quite subdued, almost timidly, he puts forward his personal reaction to what Hananiah has claimed to be God's word. "Amen," he says, "may what you say only come true! I for my part would also be glad indeed if Jerusalem's catastrophe could be averted as quickly as you say."

But then Jeremiah ventures a first word of criticism: "Yet listen, you and all the people! The prophets who were before me and before you generally prophesied disaster, war, famine, or pestilence." So Jeremiah draws on *tradition* as a preliminary guideline. He makes the people look back—as we are trying to do here, too—to the history of God's people and their prophets. Jeremiah is no doubt thinking of the great prophets of the previous two or three centuries—Elijah and Elisha, Amos and Hosea, Isaiah and Micah. These forerunners in the prophetic office were zealous in exposing sin and injustice. Accordingly, it was above all God's *judgment* that they proclaimed. Jeremiah sees the prophet's responsibility as belonging to this line of tradition. His forerunners never, as a general rule, said what people wanted to hear. They confronted their listeners extremely critically.

This is the first mark of distinction for us to bear in mind when we are trying to distinguish true prophecy from false. We must initially take a skeptical view of anyone who suppresses personal guilt or the calamity caused by guilt when he is judging present-day problems in the light of the future and in obedience to God's will; or if he fails to make the question of right and wrong one of the criteria for his decisions about the present and his expectations about the future.

Jeremiah then goes on to say, "The prophets who predicted salvation were always recognized by the fact that their predictions were fulfilled." In the situation of 593 B.C. this meant, in practical terms: at the present moment we have no sign or indication that would enable us to be certain of the authenticity of Hananiah's promise of salvation; the only thing to do is to wait. But early readers of the biblical account knew, and we today who are familiar with the sequel to the story know too that Hananiah's self-confident prediction was a deception and that Jeremiah's disputed saying was fulfilled.

But let us notice too how the false prophet Hananiah reacts to Jeremiah's interjection. He feels even more sure of himself than before, just as the prophet Zedekiah did when he was facing Micaiah ben Imlah. Hananiah lays hands on the yoke which Jeremiah is still wearing and breaks it with demonstrative force in full view of everyone, saying, "Thus says the Lord: Even so will I break the yoke of Nebuchadnezzar before two years have passed." The account then concludes movingly, "But Jeremiah the prophet went his way." He departs from the scene like a whipped puppy.

A true prophet? Yes, this is what can happen to a true prophet. Jeremiah is a man who *suffers*. He cannot act out of his own strength and he cannot, simply of his own accord, simply proclaim a divine word as Hananiah does so slickly. He has to wait in silence.

It is only after some time has elapsed (Jer. 42:7 talks about a waiting period of ten days) that he receives a new word from the Lord. This applies directly to Hananiah: "Thus says the Lord: You have broken the wooden yoke, but I will make instead a yoke of iron. All these nations will be subjected to Nebuchadnezzar. But you, Hananiah, listen! The Lord has not sent you. You have delivered up the people to deception. I will remove you from the face of the earth. This very year you shall die. For you have turned this people away from the Lord." The account closes laconically: "And the prophet Hananiah died in that same year, in the seventh month."

Let us notice from this story that the false prophet always has something to say on his own account, without any prompting, and makes a thoroughly confident impression. The true prophet has to wait for the voice of his God and is forced to endure periods of uncertainty.

Up to now these scenes from Jeremiah's life have drawn our attention to two criteria that can help us to decide between the true and the false prophetic word. The first is that we should pay attention to the great examples of history: the classic prophets are intent on detecting *guilt*, nor do they withhold the threat of *judgment*. The false prophet, on the other hand, makes things easier for his listeners. The second point is that the true prophet shows no trace of *self-confidence*. He depends solely on the assurance which his God never fails to give him as he hearkens to the divine word. He endures the periods of waiting, which are times of trial—times, too, of temptation—in which he is exposed to the scorn of his fellows.

The first two distinguishing marks are therefore (1) the pointer to a deserved judgment, and (2) the prophet's lack of self-confidence. But, as well as these, I note three other aids in the

Old Testament texts which may help us to find our bearings if we remember them in times of decision.

We find a third characteristic, for example, in the prophet Micah of Moreshet (Mic. 3:5). He talks about "the prophets who lead my people astray. When they get something to eat they cry 'salvation,' but if someone does not give them what they want, they begin to quarrel with him." Now the false prophet is recognized by his relationship to his listeners. He makes himself and his message *dependent on the favor of his listeners.* What he says is not determined by what is discernibly the will of God; it is conditioned by what people give him or fail to give him. False prophets trim their sails according to the people around them, from whom they expect some advantage or other; and they choose their texts and subjects accordingly. Micah says of them, "It shall be night to you, without vision—darkness, without divination." "There is no longer any answer from God for them" (Mic. 3:6f.). The person who ceases to ask what the will of God is when he preaches, but tries to find out what his listeners want to hear, will discover that for him God is dumb and no longer has any word.

Where this third characteristic—dependency on one's listeners —is concerned, Jeremiah is even blunter (Jer. 23:14): "They encourage evil so that no one turns away from his wickedness." Or Jer. 23:22: "If they would proclaim my words to my people, says the Lord, they would turn them from their evil way." False prophets like to humor people. They are real after-dinner speakers. Micah says in brutally coarse terms (Mic. 2:11): "If a man should utter wind and lies, saying 'I will preach to you about wine and whiskey,' he would be the preacher for this people." He would please nearly everyone. But the true witness cannot avoid practical questions about what the obedience of faith requires of us. In our own time these would be questions about our specific contribution to peace or the protection of creation. Dependency on his listeners is the third mark of a false prophet.

The fourth characteristic might be called *the ethical criterion.* In the Sermon on the Mount Jesus said quite simply and clearly (Matt. 7:15f.): "Beware of false prophets! . . . You will know them by their fruits." Jeremiah is quite precise about this point. He takes as an example two pieces of rotten fruit, which are signs of a false prophet (Jer. 23:14): "Among the prophets of Jerusalem I have seen horrible things: they commit adultery and deal with lies." The way a prophet treats his wife and his sincerity of speech make Jeremiah decide whether he is reliable in general and therefore reliable also in his prophetic office, or whether he abandons himself to license. A tree can be recognized by its fruits. Anyone who deceives his wife or his fellow human beings shows that he is a cheat. The ethical criterion tests the honesty of a person's public judgments against his evident, practical behavior.

The fifth and last criterion which I find in the Bible really embraces all the others. It might be called the *charismatic criterion.* The prophet Jeremiah distinguishes the people who lay claim to a divine word from those who are sent with a word by God himself. It is in his God's name that Jeremiah says about the false prophets (Jer. 23:21): "I did not send the prophets, yet they ran; I did not speak to them, yet they prophesied." Ezek. 13:3 talks about "the foolish prophets who follow their own spirit." In a similar way Jeremiah distinguishes the dreamers from the messengers equipped with the word of God (Jer. 23:28): "Let the prophet who has a dream tell the dream, but let him who has my word speak my word faithfully." Jeremiah warns his listeners against the prophets who "speak visions out of their own minds and not from the mouth of the Lord" (Jer. 23:16). So he continually distinguishes sharply between the individual mind or heart or individual dreams and visions on the one hand, and the word and counsel of the Lord on the other. Words that spring from the individual heart and from individual dreams and from the individual mind all issue from individual wishes and fears. Jeremiah knows from his own experience how very differently the word of the Lord confronts his spokesman. He describes (Jer. 23:9) what happens to him when God's word falls upon him and he becomes aware that it is indeed the divine word: "My heart breaks in my breast, all my bones shake, I am like a drunken man, like a man who is overcome by wine—before the Lord and before his holy words." The wishes and will of the true prophet are broken, and even his own fear is overpowered by another will outside himself, the will of God. Jeremiah, tender and sensitive as he is, is shaken even physically as he comes to feel literally "in his bones" that he is no longer obeying his own will or striving toward his own self-centered objectives. The word transforms its messenger. When the messenger is a false one, the message is more likely to concur with natural human tendencies. At all events, the willful heart is certainly to be distinguished from the heart that hears and obeys.

This final, charismatic criterion suggests particularly that initially only a true, inspired prophet can see through and expose the false one; and even he can only do so through an authority which is continually conferred on him anew. We saw this from the confrontation between Hananiah and Jeremiah. For who would claim to know, on his own account, from the external, spoken word alone, whether it simply corresponds to the natural disposition and desires of human beings or whether it is in conformity with the divine will? Only a true prophet can really see through a false one.

But how then, since we are not endowed with prophetic charisma, are *we* to judge and decide? One factor that may help us to arrive at a right decision is that, as a general rule, two different witnesses confront one another. We are always faced with two opponents, as we saw with Zedekiah and Micaiah or Hananiah and Jeremiah. Adolf Schlatter once said, in his interpretation of the Sermon on the Mount, "The lie can never resemble the truth entirely. The wolf and the sheep can always be distinguished, so that we are never completely at the mercy of any seductive power." *Comparison* therefore has to be practiced. Here the biblical prototypes and one or the other of the five distinguishing criteria can be of help to us. We always have to ask ourselves who is most like the true prophet and who is closest to the false. But above all we must inquire who reminds us more clearly of Jesus Christ, of what he said and did, of his suffering, and of his continuing workings in the Spirit.

Let us, in closing, try to apply these tests to the general subject of our situation today and to the prophecy about the possible catastrophe threatening the whole humanity in the age of nuclear armaments.

Can you imagine a cube with sides about eight feet long? The rooms in our houses are generally about eight feet high. Imagine that a huge cube like this is hovering over your head. Remember that physicists have calculated that a quantity of nuclear explosives in this amount is already available for every single person in the world today, stored up in the arsenals of the major powers. True prophets today will not conceal disastrous facts like this. Even less may they hold their tongues about the vast tissue of guilt, mistrust, fear, profit-seeking, and hostility which led to, and are still leading to, these stores for the annihilation of mankind. The extinction of the nations has been prepared for with perfection and can be set in motion by pressing only a very few buttons. So what Isaiah (Isa. 1:31) once prophesied for Israel is today an entirely conceivable future for the whole world: "Then the strong will become tinder, and what he does, an inflaming spark. Both of them burn together, and no one can quench them."

The prophet Jonah once had to proclaim to the capital of the brutal Assyrian Empire: "Yet forty days, and Nineveh shall be overthrown." But, so the Book of Jonah tells us, the men of Nineveh put their trust in God, repented, and made a fresh beginning. Then God was sorry for the evil with which he had threatened them; and he did not inflict it upon them.

This ancient story about Nineveh warns us that humankind's days are numbered. We need and we pray for truthful prophets of disaster who do not try to evade their task, as Jonah vainly attempted to do. Guilt and calamity must be exposed—calamity and guilt in equal measure. For what is at work among us is not blind fate but the guilt of men and women. And God's judgment means that our own godless acts recoil on our own heads. Nineveh is a challenge to our obedient faith; the word can bring about the turning point. The word of true prophets can transform its hearers, as it has transformed its spokesman. This we have learned.

Nineveh repented. Nineveh turned away from its wickedness, and God withdrew his word of disaster. The word promising destruction which the prophets uttered was not after all fulfilled. Does this mean that it was a false prophetic word? It reached the target at which it was essentially aiming: the person who listened to it and whom it converted and saved. This is the way the mercy of God triumphs over his anger. We need and pray for true prophets of repentance whose word brings about the turning point, the turning point which will avert the universal and already possible catastrophe.

So in this hour of history we pray for a turning away from the false prophecy which is still bent on calculating the precise degree of retaliation between one political bloc and another. It is this retaliatory thinking, this thinking in terms of an equilibrium of terror and of armaments, that has cast us into the desolation in which we find ourselves on the eve of the second millennium. In the discussions about disarmament among those of us who are Germans, true prophecy will never keep silent about the appalling guilt which we especially have incurred towards Russia. We remember far too seldom that in 1941 it was we who broke the treaty we had made and began the terrible war against the Soviet Union. Almost twenty million Soviet soldiers were killed as well as seven million civilians (compared with four and one-half million Germans). In view of this overall statistical result of our invasion, who could fail to understand the Soviet fear of the West? We Germans are totally dependent on forgiveness at every level. It is only with the help of forgiveness that a new life will be possible. We must face up to a prophecy that does not repress our history of guilt or our dependence on forgiveness. There is no other possible, viable foundation, even for our political thinking.

In this hour of history we therefore pray in general that we may all turn away from a false prophecy whose policies are based on mistrust alone. In the long run we certainly cannot rely on a policy of deterrence. Every increase in our own security through nuclear weapons is also a dangerous increase in our own risk. So we pray that men and women may turn to a prophecy of peaceableness and love of our enemies. Here Jesus' command seems to be the command of the hour. We have to think it through with new intelligence, to change our behavior accordingly, and to support and encourage negotiations. We, all of us, must help to build up and expand the climate of trust. Indira Gandhi recently figured out for the North-South Conference what huge areas of desert could be made fertile with the money spent on a single long-range rocket.

So we now pray above all that there may be a turning away from the fraudulent prophecy that starts from the assumption that it is always the *other* side who must begin to show the marks of confidence. A prophecy which leaves us unchanged ourselves is certainly false. We pray for the countries of the West, especially where they claim to be Christian, that they may turn to the true policy which will encourage us to take *the first steps* in demolishing the appalling arms depots. It is this which will show where we really put our trust—in the way Jesus has shown us or in our own fear; in the securities we create for ourselves or in the one who cries to us "Fear not, for I am with you! Do not give way, for I am your God!" (Isa. 41:10).

Is this promise for us nothing more than an empty phrase? Or is it the foundation of life? Do we see how the whole future of mankind depends on the clear distinction between true and false prophecy? May God increase this clarity among us, through Jesus Christ.

SCRIPTURE INDEX

OLD TESTAMENT

Genesis
19:25—32

Exodus
20:17—38
20:18-19—54
24:3-8—56

Leviticus
19:13—38

Deuteronomy
6—54
6:6—55
21:18—34
21:21—32
24:1-4—24, 34
29:22—32

1 Kings
22—66

2 Chronicles
32:27-31—44

Psalms
46—46

Proverbs
17:8—46
17:23—45-46
21:13—41

Song of Solomon
2:1, 3, 16—33
4:10—33

Isaiah
1:2-3—53
1:31—74
5:20—44
10:15—53-54
14:32—45
30:15-17—63
41:10—76
43:18—62

Jeremiah
11:10—53
13:23—55
15:18—67
17:1—55
20:7—15
23:9—72
23:14—71, 72
23:16—72
23:21—72

23:22—71
23:28—72
26:17-19—36, 47
27-28—67-70
31:31-34—49
31:31—49-50, 54
31:32—50, 52-53, 60
31:33—50, 54, 56
31:34—57, 59-60
32:40—60-61
42:7—70

Lamentations
2:14—42

Ezekiel
11:19—55
13:3—72
36:26—55

Hosea
1-3—22
1:2—23
1:9—53
2:2—26
2:2-3—29
2:4-5—29
2:6-7—30

2:8—26
2:8, 13—30
2:14-15—30
3:1, 2—24, 25
4:10—27
4:13-14—26
5:4—31, 33
5:12—28
5:14—27
6:4—30
6:5—22
7:2—31, 33
7:12—27
11:1-7—31-32
11:1, 4—32
11:5—31
11:6—32
11:7—31
11:8—31
11:9—32
13:2—26
13:4—27
13:7-8—28
14:5—28
14:6-8—33
14:8—28

Amos
1:4-5, 7-8—17-18
2:2-3—18
2:6-8—19
2:13-16—19
3:2—17, 18
3:8—10
3:15—18
4:2-4—17
4:12—18
5:4—20, 21
5:17—18
5:21-24—19

5:27—18, 19
6:1-7—19
6:8—18
7:1-8—13
7:8—18
7:10-17—11
7:11—16
7:14-16—12-13, 65
7:17—17
8:1-2—13
8:2—13
9:1-4—13
9:4—18
9:11-12—20

Micah
1:1—36
2:1-11—37
2:1—38
2:3—38
2:6—38
2:7—39, 47
2:8—39
2:10—40
2:11—40, 71
3:1-4—41
3:1, 9—36
3:2-3—41, 45
3:3—45
3:4—41, 47
3:5—42, 47
3:6-7—43, 71
3:8—36
3:9-12—43-44
3:10—45
3:11—42, 45, 46,
  47, 65
3:12—47
7:19—59

NEW TESTAMENT

Matthew
7:15—64, 65
7:15-16—71
10:41—64
15:24—52
23:34—64
28:19—52

Luke
13:34-35—64
19:43—64
22:20—56
22:42—56

John
4:34—56

Acts
4:20—16

Romans
8:3—34
9:25—56
11:18—52

1 Corinthians
9:16—16

2 Corinthians
1:22—57
1:24—59
5:15—57

1 Thessalonians
5:20-21—64